D1547908

# Sun and Moon Signs

*Secrets of the 12 Zodiac Signs, Different Sun-Moon Astrology Combinations, Personality Types, and Compatibility*

## Your Free Gift (only available for a limited time)

Thanks for getting this book! If you want to learn more about various spirituality topics, then join Mari Silva's community and get a free guided meditation MP3 for awakening your third eye. This guided meditation mp3 is designed to open and strengthen ones third eye so you can experience a higher state of consciousness. Simply visit the link below the image to get started.

https://spiritualityspot.com/meditation

# Contents

# Part 1: Sun Signs

*Unlocking the Secrets of the 12 Zodiac Signs in Western Astrology to Understand Personality Types*

# Introduction

For most people, horoscopic astrology is little more than a source of entertainment and something to help pass the time. It usually ends with reading the daily horoscope over a cup of coffee or comparing it to the day's events. This is unfortunate because it doesn't even scratch the surface of what your zodiac sign can tell you about yourself and what the signs of others can tell you about them.

Everybody knows their astrological sign of the zodiac, and most people will, at some point, discuss their signs with someone as a form of small talk, but that's usually as far as the interest goes. One common misconception about zodiac signs and the horoscope is that they are about fortune-telling. In reality, there is much more than meets the eye when it comes to your zodiac sign. One of the most important things about the twelve zodiac signs is how they relate to personality types and how they can help us understand people and their feelings and actions better.

The first step toward getting a better understanding of zodiac signs is learning that there are three groups, including sun signs, which we will discuss in this book, and moon signs and rising signs, also known as ascendant signs. Each person has one sign in each of these three classifications, and the most committed astrologers will use all three to come up with the most detailed profile of a person.

Sun sign astrology, which focuses on the twelve sun signs of the zodiac, is essentially a simplified way of doing things, characteristic of Western astrology.

That doesn't mean it's not a sophisticated system, though. Western astrology is rooted in ancient Mesopotamia and Greece, and, as such, it is over 2,000 years old. The Babylonians and the Greeks are the most credited cultures when it comes to the early development of the system, but others have also done an important part in preserving it, such as the Romans and Arabs. Much of what has been preserved from old Hellenistic astrology is owed to the records kept by Ptolemy, a Roman mathematician, astronomer, astrologer, and geographer, in the 2nd century AD. This is now known as Western astrology and is widely used.

In that regard, astrological signs are the twelve signs that represent 30-degree sectors of the ecliptic (the plane of the earth's orbit around the sun). The signs begin at something called the *vernal equinox* with the sign of Aries. Without going into too much detail, the signs are based on individual constellations visible within the zodiac. This is the name that's been given to a particular belt or area we can observe in the sky, eight degrees north or south of the ecliptic.

This is the path of the sun across the *celestial sphere* in the course of a year or, more precisely, the tropical year which is the time it takes for the sun to find its way back to the same position. This relates to what we can observe from here on Earth. Within that same zodiac belt, we can observe the paths of the moon and planets, all of which are important for Western astrology. What the zodiac itself is and all the astronomical details that play a part in astrology deserve a book of their own, though. This book will focus on the practical ways these different factors might affect us on a personal level. Before we delve into the twelve signs, let's clear up a few more things about what the different signs are and what additional aspects, characteristics, and classifications of these signs astrologers use to get a clear picture of a person's birth chart - and how it affects them.

When a person is born, the stars, planets, and the sun will be in certain positions when observed from Earth, which will determine that person's *natal chart.* This is how a person's sun, moon, and rising signs are identified.

As we briefly mentioned, the sun sign is the one that everyone knows. As its name suggests, the sun sign is determined by the zodiac sign in which the sun can be observed on your birth date. In each sign, the sun relates to the Earth differently, affecting us all. In some signs, the sun is further away or is visible for fewer hours a day, while in others, our life-sustaining star is at its most powerful and radiant. Based on these and other properties related to each of the twelve signs, we are given certain traits and characteristics at birth - exactly what *sun sign astrology* studies.

The position of the moon determines your moon sign. This sign influences the subtler, hidden side of your nature and identity. The moon sign can influence your emotional characteristics, especially those that you can't always express - those that remain hidden. Think of stuff like your inner monologue, thoughts, intuition, and other things we all hear in our minds and hearts.

The rising or ascendant signs are perhaps the ones you hear the least about. Your rising sign can most aptly be described as the *social you,* and it's the one that was on the eastern horizon at your time of birth. The sign is the social you because it is the manifestation of how you present yourself to the world. Virtually everyone does this to some extent: they dress a certain way, adopt styles, and choose which bits of their real personality they want to reveal. The things you choose to show tell a lot about you and your priorities, so many astrologers think this is an important sign to consider.

Your sun sign will be enough to determine your sign's core traits. There are many reasons it's important to understand the signs of the zodiac, especially your sun sign. For one, you will get a better understanding of your strengths and weaknesses while also learning how to make the most of them. You will gain the same insight into other people, which will help you deal with conflict in a healthier way, empathize more, and improve your existing relationships.

### Elements

As we explore the details and traits of each of the twelve signs, it will become much clearer how the elements, modality, and other classifications come into play. For now, let us start by pointing out there are four elements, including fire, earth, air, and water. These elements are equal in importance and power, but they all rule different areas and have unique characters. These four elements are also called *the classical elements* because they were identified and described by Empedocles, a Greek philosopher in the 5th century BC.

Each of the twelve zodiac signs is imbued with one of these four elements - and those four are equally distributed among the twelve. The signs' elemental classifications are further divided into two groups according to their polarity, with fire and air signs being positive while water and earth signs are negative. Among the positive signs, fire signs include Aries, Leo, and Sagittarius, while air signs include Gemini, Libra, and Aquarius. As for the negative signs, earth signs are Taurus, Virgo, and Capricorn, while Cancer, Scorpio, and Pisces have water as their element. As we explore the different signs, we will consider how the respective elements influence each sign.

### Modality

Among the four elements, each includes three modalities, which are cardinal, fixed, and mutable. Each modality influences four signs and determines a lot about their nature. Cardinal signs are Aries, Cancer, Libra, and Capricorn. These signs are also called reacting or reactive signs. The name of this class of signs suggests that they are "important," symbolized by the fact that each sign marks the start of a new season.

As for the fixed-modality signs, these include Taurus, Leo, Scorpio, and Aquarius. The fixed modality is associated with stability, strong will, depth, and other characteristics. One way the fixed modality affects these signs is by making them resistant to change, but you will learn later how that translates to personal traits in each sign.

Finally, there are four mutable signs, including Gemini, Virgo, Sagittarius, and Pisces. Mutable modality has the opposite influence on that of fixed modality largely. These signs are adaptable and flexible, among other things. These signs love to experience and influence change. What's also important for these signs is that they each mark the end of a season.

### Planetary Rulership

Each of the twelve zodiac signs is ruled by at least one planet in the solar system. In the simplest terms, these are the special relationships that the zodiac signs have with celestial bodies in our system. When a person is born under a certain sign, the position of these planets can influence them in various ways. In Western astrology, each sign has classical and modern ruling planets, which are the same in all but three cases, these being Scorpio, Aquarius, and Pisces. Furthermore, each planet has its own properties and traits, usually embodied in the gods of many past mythologies. Planetary rulership for each sign is:

- Aries - Mars
- Taurus - Venus
- Gemini - Mercury
- Cancer - Moon
- Leo - Sun

- Virgo - Mercury
- Libra - Venus
- Scorpio - Pluto (Modern) and Mars (Classical)
- Sagittarius - Jupiter
- Capricorn - Saturn
- Aquarius - Uranus (Modern) and Saturn (Classical)
- Pisces - Neptune (Modern) and Jupiter (Classical)

Regarding planets, there are other factors that astrologers will consider when looking at an individual's birth chart. For instance, a planet can be exalted or in detriment in certain signs. Rulership is not to be misunderstood as meaning that a planet is guaranteed to be in a certain sign. When a planet is in a sign in which it's said to be in detriment, it will be in a weakened state, meaning it can't reach its full potential and will ultimately have a detrimental influence on the person born under such a placement. But a planet will be exalted when placed in its home sign (domicile), which means it will be strongest. You will learn more about this later in this book.

**Houses**

The last thing to clear up before we begin is astrological houses, which is another system of dividing the horoscope, this time into twelve parts. The positions of these houses are determined by physical location and time of day instead of a date. As such, houses are another important factor that astrologers consider when creating someone's natal chart. The classification is rather simple, outlining twelve houses from the first to the twelfth, all of which correspond to the twelve zodiac signs. The following is a list of the astrological houses, their corresponding zodiac signs, and one respective variation of their title, each:

- The First House - Aries - House of Self
- The Second House - Taurus - House of Value

- The Third House - Gemini - House of Sharing
- The Fourth House - Cancer - House of Home and Family
- The Fifth House - Leo - House of Pleasure
- The Sixth House - Virgo - House of Health
- The Seventh House - Libra - House of Balance
- The Eighth House - Scorpio - House of Transformation
- The Ninth House - Sagittarius - House of Philosophy
- The Tenth House - Capricorn - House of Enterprise
- The Eleventh House - Aquarius - House of Blessings
- The Twelfth House - Pisces - House of Sacrifice

# Chapter One: Aries – The Ram

Experimentation, boldness, independence, honor, and initiative are the most pronounced traits that mark Aries' nature. Aries is a fire sign ruled by Mars while it rules the first house, which are aspects that determine the sign's fiery and headstrong nature. This is why Aries' astrological symbol, which is the ram, is so fitting.

Although Aries is the first of the twelve zodiac signs, the sign's date of birth falls approximately between March 21 and April 19. The ram's modality is cardinal, which determines many of their distinct traits, especially those that impact the way they relate to others. Like the other three cardinal signs, Aries marks the beginning of a new season. Since that season is spring, this is generally interpreted as one of the sources of Aries' high levels of energy, motivation, and leadership skills. But Aries's fire element fuels the sign's other characteristics, such as assertiveness, passion, and occasional impulsiveness.

While Mars rules it, Aries is also under the influence of many other planets in different ways. For instance, according to the Thema Mundi, the old Hellenic birth chart, Aries is positioned on the chart's midheaven (top). According to this interpretation, this position places Aries so it ensures it gets the most power out of the sun. Aries also has a modern, secondary ruler represented by Pluto, just like other signs, as you'll learn later. Detrimental influence can occur when Venus or Saturn is in Aries. As such, Aries' detriment planet is primarily Venus, while its exalted celestial body is the sun itself.

## Personality Traits

Folks born under the sign of Aries tend to be hard-chargers, making them strong leaders and making their presence known everywhere they go. They are often imposing characters with a lot of energy and charisma, which rubs off on the people they encounter. This impression can be positive or negative, depending on various contexts and the traits of the people they interact with.

Aries is the person who always prefers to take the initiative, break new ground, and open the path for others. This also means they are very independent-minded and self-reliant while, at the same time, usually being led by a strong sense of honor. Because of this sign's cardinal modality, Aries also tends to be traditional and easy to reason with. Because of their combination of leadership and courage, rams are the folks who chart the path and dare to tread where others haven't. This also means that Aries are risk-takers, which often translates into success in many walks of life. Their courage is owed to the rule of Mars. Aries are generally folks with a very positive outlook on life, having the optimism and faith to always think of a way to solve a problem and the persistence to keep trying until a successful outcome or until they run out of options.

Despite their capacity to be reasonable, but the ram's hard-charging, courageous nature can sometimes make them a little too quick to act. In the simplest terms, Aries is known to be quick-tempered. Verbal and even physical outbursts are highly likely occasionally. Even though their reason is quick to kick in and calm them down, and although rams rarely hold grudges, their outbursts can sometimes cause severe damage to their relationships. Another potential Aries flaw concerns their willingness to take risks.

When unchecked and unhinged, the ram's optimism and courage can lead them down dangerous roads, both physically and metaphorically. Rams are also often impatient and restless, which can translate to various difficulties. Many Aries will find it difficult to stick with one thing, whether it's a task, a leisurely activity, or anything else. Often, an Aries will want to move on to something more stimulating before they're done with whatever they have been working on.

## Compatibility

The compatibility of Aries with other Aries leaves a fair amount to be desired. Primarily because of their similarity, Aries are often not very compatible with each other in love, but there can be exceptions. Similarities can also be a solid basis for friendship or other forms of cooperation, so there are undoubtedly contexts where Aries and Aries can function properly.

As for the other signs, Aries will find that some are very agreeable, while others might give them significant difficulty. Generally, Aries is the most compatible with Virgo, Sagittarius, and Pisces, especially in romantic relationships. The compatibility with the other signs varies in how difficult it is for Aries to get along, but most relationships work out with enough understanding and effort.

Despite the things that can sometimes go wrong, Aries' nature makes them very sociable, and they are usually well-liked. Because they are outgoing and communicative, rams are fun, and their energy has a way of rubbing off on other people. As dominant as they might be, Aries folks are still magnanimous and, as we mentioned, honorable. Often, this makes them very good partners, friends, coworkers, and acquaintances.

Aries can run into problems with people with little patience for their high levels of energy and their imposing character. Those who are rebellious by nature can get defensive if they sense that the Aries' domineering personality is a threat to their independence or pride. Such encounters can be especially problematic if an Aries has fallen into a few traps you've read about. In extreme cases, Aries can become too bossy or even turn into bullies. When they run into folks who want to assert themselves and push back, serious conflicts can erupt.

## Love

The ram's headstrong, courageous, and fiery nature is usually quite pronounced in their love life and can come as either shocking or refreshing to the other party. If you're a ram, then you are likely to have experienced this drive already. Like elsewhere in life, Aries has no problem getting into a relationship, even if it entails risk or involves a lot of uncharted territories. They will give things a chance and try to make it work, especially if they feel strongly about a person.

Once in a relationship with someone, the ram's unrestrained openness will continue. Aries will clearly, loudly, and fearlessly express their feelings, and their approach will be the same with commitment because they aren't afraid to get serious about a person. This all makes Aries very passionate in love and can provide for many romantic moments. What's more, the person who experiences this onslaught of love from Aries will feel like they are at the top of the world. Some signs will enjoy that, but others who are more concerned about consequences and prefer to think in the long term might get to feeling uncomfortable with Aries' relentless onward charge.

On the flip side, this uninhibited approach can also lead to a fair bit of blindness, which can be a hurtful and dangerous thing in love. This can eventually lead to problems not just for other people but also for Aries themselves. Aries has that rational side, but, as we mentioned earlier, their headstrong, hard-charging nature can often overcome. The things the ram says to a partner and the openness of their emotions can feed that other person's blind love. This is especially likely to happen when the relationship is between two rams. That's why Aries can greatly benefit from a calculated and highly rational partner, but when all is said and done, Aries will make a highly dynamic, passionate, honest, and fun partner.

## Other Relationships

Aries' loyalty is what makes them very adept at all sorts of relationships other than romantic ones. Rams make great friends and are usually very devoted to their family. This is true even when it doesn't translate into a functioning relationship. Aries can get caught up in their worldly pursuits and unwittingly neglect the people who matter for some time before they check in again.

In Aries' mind, nothing is wrong, and the situation is normal, but other signs can take this distance to heart. But under the surface, Aries will have no doubt as to where their loyalties lie. Aries is a fiery sign that can get heated and blow a fuse quickly. This temper can hinder relationships, especially with their family members. Not seeing eye-to-eye with parents, siblings, and other loved ones can set Aries off and lead to conflict. Again, though, Aries will remain loyal and, when push comes to shove, they will be there for their loved ones.

If you have Aries children, you must consider the traits that we've discussed from an early age. These children are outgoing, proactive, and they will aim to assert themselves among peers. An Aries child should be taught discipline from as early as possible because this nature can lead an undisciplined Aries child into much trouble. On the flip side of that coin, Aries makes passionately devoted parents, but their temper can be a problem. Children that require a calculated, patient approach can suffer if their Aries parent doesn't learn to be less reactive, especially when they are too quick to apply punishment.

Finally, Aries won't have a lot of difficulties in making friends wherever they go. Aries being a fiery, thrill-seeking individual who needs change and spontaneity, their friends must know how to keep up to keep the friendship going.

## Work

Aries' perfect professions are those where their individuality, self-reliance, confidence, risk-taking, and desire for thrills can all be fully realized. Careers that aren't stimulating and dynamic can feel like a prison sentence for Aries. Above all, Aries should avoid jobs that entail a lot of routines and require a person to spend a lot of time on small details. The only way Aries can hold this type of job and maintain a semblance of fulfillment is by compensating with copious amounts of adventure, exercise, and excitement in their personal life outside of work.

As you can probably deduce, Aries folks tend to be right at home in the military, police, or other high-intensity jobs. It's not just that these jobs are stimulating and intense, though. Aries craves the simple and clear purpose these jobs can provide, and often, they will enjoy fighting under that purpose. Other emergency services are also natural callings for Aries, whether it's firefighters, emergency medical personnel, or rescue services.

Aries will also do well when they dedicate their life to highly competitive sports, especially boxing, martial arts, and wrestling. These disciplines give Aries ample opportunity to fight and do so with integrity while also striving to be the best version of themselves, physically and mentally. Mars, usually treated as the god of war, influences the affinities in Aries.

In the workplace, Aries will shine with their gift of leadership, and they will have no problem asserting themselves. If they don't slip into any of their negative extremes, Aries folks can make outstanding supervisors of all sorts. They will have the confidence to lead, but more important, they will have the understanding and willingness to help and counsel their subordinates. Aries has the potential to be the best bosses ever. If they lose their balance and succumb to those potential flaws, though, they can be a nightmare to work with, let alone work under.

## Getting Along with an Aries

To get along with an Aries, it's important to have respect, be honest, and have a thick skin. As you've read, Aries can be very honest, quick-tempered, and dominant. When combined, these factors can make them say and do harsh things they might regret later. To get along with Aries, but you must be prepared for such incidents. It will be important that you react rationally but also assertively, all while not adding your own fuel to the fire. Aries will respect you for holding your own, but he or she will also see reason more easily if you keep a clear head and stay in control.

It's also a good idea to let Aries decide on the details of your plans, such as the time and place of a meeting, for instance. It's not a matter of feeding their ego, though. Let them take charge because they are usually the most adventurous person in the room. Plus, Aries is at their best when taking charge, so you are likely to have more fun with them than you would otherwise.

Your best bet is to keep an open mind and try to be flexible. For getting along with an Aries, nature will luckily be on your side. These folks are simply easy to get along with by their very personality. If you can keep up with the excitement and the energy, you will find you need not do anything special. Most of the time, Aries will befriend you or establish communication before you've even had time to plan out your approach. It's just what they do.

# Chapter Two: Taurus – The Bull

If Aries is a fan of challenges and enjoys the rush of getting into a new one, Taurus is the person who focuses on the rewards that the challenge might bring. If you are a Taurus, you are likely a diligent and goal-oriented person strongly focusing on getting as much enjoyment from life as possible. With a birth range between April 20 and May 20, Taurus is the second sign of the zodiac, and it is associated with the second house. Represented by the bull constellation, the sign of Taurus is ruled by Venus, its element is earth, and its modality is fixed.

Taureans' distinct characteristics include intelligence, diligence, dedication, stubbornness, dependability, and work ethic. Taurus' fixed modality blesses those born under the sign with stability that can manifest in many ways, varying from one person to the next. Taurus is the first of four fixed signs, all of which occupy a place in the middle of each of the four seasons. The sign's earth element, being the most solid and firm of the four, is what infuses Taurus with things like patience, dependability, and consistency.

Taurus' Venus domicile influences Taurean's inclination toward accumulation and the creation of all those things that please them. The second house, also known as the house of value or the house of security and wealth, has a lot to do with the priorities that

Taureans set for themselves in life. Taurus can come under some detrimental influence if Mars enters the sign, particularly by taking some of Taurus' traits into a harmful extreme. Taurus' stability can thus turn into too much tolerance and eventually make them complacent. This can affect both their interaction with people and their outlook on life, affecting things like motivation, outspokenness, and a willingness to tackle problems.

## Personality Traits

Taurus is typically the person who knows how to live a good life, so to speak. These are folks who have a high appreciation for all those finer things in life that make our existence more comfortable. Physical pleasures, material goods, overall comfort, and satisfaction of their sophisticated taste are only a few things that people born under Taurus's sign will seek in their lives. Simply put, the reward is one of the most important things for a Taurus.

That's not to say that Taurus's expect life's rewards and pleasures to come freely - quite the contrary. If you are a Taurus, you probably are a hard worker. People born under this sign are not reluctant to put the work in, and they are very meticulous, practical, and dedicated to their obligations. Another common trait found in Taurus people is that they are down-to-earth. This means that it's difficult for them to get carried away and lost in fantasies or unrealistic ideals. As such, a Taurus is focused on the here-and-now and on getting the job done.

Stability in its many manifestations is an important part of Taurus' character. Sometimes called the "anchor of the zodiac," bulls tend to be consistent and reliable. Honesty is another positive trait that most Taureans have but also expect from others.

As for negative traits, a Taurus can go awry when some traits that can otherwise be viewed as virtues go to the extreme. As such, Taureans have been known to be too stubborn. Some are prone to obsessive behavior when their commitment and dedication leave the realm of rationality. Of course, their love of pleasure and comfort is something else that can end quite badly if it goes too far, particularly when it turns into the greed of unrestrained hedonism.

## Compatibility

Taurus' compatibility is at its best when they are dealing with earth and water signs. Water signs complement Taureans with emotional sophistication and a healthy dose of vulnerability, which translates to openness when it is within reason. In a relationship between Taurus and Cancer, for instance, Cancer's nurturing personality will be very healthy for the Taurean. On the other hand, Cancer will appreciate Taurus' dependability and support. With Pisces, Taurus' life will be enriched by spirituality and philosophy, elevating the bull's overall awareness. With this influence, Taureans can leave their comfort zone in new, highly productive ways. In return, the bull will provide Pisces with grounding to keep them from losing sight of reality when they delve into their abstraction. Taurus can also enjoy a very fulfilling romantic relationship with Scorpio, especially regarding sexuality.

With earth signs, Taureans will get along very well with other folks under the same signs. Their greatest agreement will be regarding lifestyle and enjoyment of worldly comforts. Virgo is another sign with which Taurus can have a great and highly complementary relationship. The indulgent Taurean will benefit from Virgo's health advice, while the bull's life philosophy can rub off on Virgo and alleviate some of this sign's anxieties. The constructive and authoritative Capricorn is materially oriented, just like Taurus. These two signs will work together well toward a common, material goal, but both signs are also rather sensual, so there is a lot of potential for intimacy.

Taureans might enjoy the energetic nature of fire signs for a while, but they will eventually tire of the volatility and potential instability these signs might bring into life. The Aries' impatience, Sagittarius' yearning for frequent change, and Leo's stubbornness can often be too much for the stable and grounded Taurus.

Similarly, air signs can prove way too fast and restless for the bull. The methodical Taurus appreciates consistency and order, which they are unlikely to get from the often-hectic Gemini. Because Venus rules both, Taurus and Libra will share certain interests. Libra's propensity for spontaneity, but is a fundamental difference between the two. Aquarius is another sign that Taureans might get along. They probably won't though in the long run, mostly because of a conflict between their value systems.

## Love

Since Taurus' ruling planet, Venus, is also the goddess of love, this zodiac sign does well in romantic relationships. Among other things, this influence makes most Taurus folks romantic, or at least appreciative of romance. Taurus' adeptness at relationship is about much more than just a propensity for romantic moments, though. Another great contributor to their success in this field is their honesty.

Bulls are also meticulous and diligent in love, just like in everything else, and this applies not just to maintain their relationships but also to start them. Unlike Aries, a Taurus will never let excitement get the better of them and make them rush blindly into anything, least of all a romantic relationship. Even in matters of love, Taureans tend to maintain their rationality and be the voice of reason. When a Taurus doesn't see the potential in a relationship proposal, he or she will act on that concern. This will often come across as cold, but it can save both the Taurus and the other person a lot of trouble in the long run.

Even after they get into a relationship, Taureans will keep using the brakes, and they will take things slow. If you find yourself in a relationship with a Taurus, and he or she seems distant at first, it's important to keep in mind that they simply take time to open up and consolidate the connection. Once they do, you will find that a Taurus' honesty, loyalty, and commitment will make for a reliable, loving partner who gets into relationships for the long run. Unlike other signs such as Aries, who tend to get restless staying in one place for too long, a Taurus will cherish their relationship.

The bull will draw satisfaction from working to build that relationship into something that gets ever-stronger. The only problem is that, sometimes, Taureans might fall victim to perfectionism and set unrealistic expectations not just for their partner but for human relationships as a whole.

## Other Relationships

Taurus' dependability, stability, and trustworthiness are qualities that make them excellent friends. They usually take time to get comfortable and personal with someone new, but once a meaningful connection and trust are established, Taurus will open up and demonstrate the true meaning of friendship and loyalty. Taurus will be the friend who need not hang out with you every night, but if you call needing urgent help, your Taurean friend will be there at 3 AM if necessary.

Taurus' well-intentioned, honest nature makes their friendship valuable in a way you can't get from other folks, no matter how fun they might be. Taurus won't lie to you to make you feel comfortable, for instance. Instead, he or she will give you their honest opinion and advice, all of which will help you grow as a person.

Many of the Taurean virtues will certainly be valuable in workplace relationships, especially reliability, honesty, and stability. Taurus is the last person who will get into petty office drama, talk behind your back, or bother with other schemes. The Taurean will be too busy focusing on their work and making sure they are getting the job done right. As such, Taurus is the person to go to for advice, guidance, and for entrusting important, complex projects.

People who value diligence, hard work, and a no-nonsense attitude will have no problems with a Taurean coworker, even though they prefer to work independently. If a team is cohesive, well-organized, and runs like a clock, Taurus will certainly have no problem fitting in. Since Taurus loves to unwind after a hard day's work and indulges in worldly comforts, they will also be more than willing to partake in fun times with their colleagues.

## Work

The methodical Taurus is at his or her best when assigned to one big project that requires long-term dedication, planning, and focus. Taureans will enjoy building, both physically and mentally, but they do usually enjoy work that requires a more hands-on approach. Taureans also doesn't shy away from routine, at least to a certain degree. What they thrive on is structure and consistency, which a routine can provide, but if it's on the wrong job, the bull will find it difficult to get excited about their work.

Taurus would probably do poorly in a work environment that Aries would enjoy. Taureans prefer as little chaos and distractions as possible in their workspace. If you have a job requiring a long, thorough, concentrated approach, give that job to Taurus. Remember that Taurus also relishes in rewards, so the longer and more difficult a job is, the more they will enjoy the reward at the end. The job or the feeling of having done it can be rewarded in and of themselves for Taurus. Taureans usually enjoy jobs that require them to care for others because they are stable individuals good at giving support to those in need.

Because of their love of quiet environments and their earthy nature, Taureans also enjoy working in outdoor, natural environments. Gardening, farming, and ranching are other jobs and lifestyles that Taureans enjoy immensely. Trades like carpentry are also virtually perfect for Taureans because they allow them to work with their hands, take their time, and focus on their work in the quiet comfort of their work shed.

## Getting Along with a Taurus

Getting along with a Taurus largely revolves around knowing how to approach and get closer to them. If you were born under one of the other signs, a Taurus might seem difficult to relate to, but that's just because they have a strict filter that determines who is and isn't allowed into their life, but with a bit of effort, it won't be too difficult to learn that they are a normal and relatable person.

A great place to start is to find common ground, and the best way to do that with a Taurus is to remember that they are people who work and play hard. Participating in the same work project or sharing professional interests are good ways to bond with a Taurus. They also tend to bond well with those who accompany them when having a good time and unwinding. Since Taureans ascribe so much importance to enjoyment and pleasure, they usually form strong, pleasant memories of such experiences. Finding your way into those memories is a great way to inch closer to a Taurus' heart.

Taureans will also sometimes use their own vetting system to determine who should be allowed into their lives and who shouldn't. Many such Taureans will do this without even thinking about it, since it comes naturally to them, but others will have an intricate system of questions and subtle little tests they knowingly use whenever they meet someone new. Most people won't even be aware that they are being tested and evaluated, but the bull will be picking up important pieces of information that will help them determine whether you are up to the standards they expect from people looking to become their friends or something more.

Once you establish any relationship with a Taurus, you must remember that they can be stubborn. If a Taurean believes that they are right about something, they won't just change their tune to make their friend or partner feel more comfortable. Without strong argumentation, a Taurus' mind can hardly be changed.

# Chapter Three: Gemini – The Twins

The third sign's astrological symbol, the twins, is befitting because it hints at Gemini's nature, which can come across as dual to other people. Sometimes, that nature can appear to be even more complicated than just dual because Geminis can be the most incomprehensible folks out there, particularly from the perspective of other signs. This is because with traits, Geminis have the widest and most variable range. Of all the signs in the zodiac, Gemini is the most difficult to define due to a frequent lack of that one definitive trait that other signs usually have. Whereas you can usually tell an Aries by their leadership skills, a Gemini can come as quite a surprise.

The Gemini season falls between May 21 and June 21 and is ruled by Mercury. Gemini is associated with the third house and is an air sign of mutable modality. The sign's association with the third house is what conditions Gemini's intellectual and curious nature when such is manifested.

Being the first of the mutable signs is what makes Gemini adaptable and prone to change, as is appropriate for a sign that occupies a transitional time between spring and summer. Just as nature restlessly strives to bloom and achieve its maximum during this time, Gemini seeks change and novelty. Gemini's nature is also reflected in elemental air, which is flowing, active, and difficult to define. Like air, Gemini wants to be everywhere and experience everything at once, if only they could. Gemini's ruling planet, too, resembles the nature of the Twins, being very fast and retrograde more often than any other planet in the Solar System. As such, Mercury in Gemini has a lot to do with the sign's restlessness, curiosity, quick absorption of new information, and wit.

## Personality Traits

As you've just read, Geminis can be quite variable by nature. Still, a few Gemini strengths and weaknesses can be outlined, which will often apply to the Geminis you might run into. Overall, that of the most common Gemini traits include adaptability, openness, and intelligence, but sometimes also indecisiveness, unreliability, and impulsiveness. The curiosity can lead a Gemini on a path to becoming overly nosy. Their nosiness can combine with unreliability and an inclination toward gossiping, which makes Geminis not very good to confide in. This is because many Geminis love to share the information that they've gathered on their eternal quest to get as clever as they can. Many simply love to talk, and they enjoy the attention they can get this way, which is why they try to collect the most interesting information they can.

One of Gemini's greatest strengths is often their adaptability. Adaptable Geminis enjoy trying new things and getting on adventures. Their occasional unreliability can be somewhat compensated for by their ability to adapt to all changes of schedule. If you must change plans suddenly, your Gemini friend will probably have no problem shuffling a few things around and getting down with the new program. As such, a Gemini can be very easy-going, laid-back, agreeable, and above all, fun.

The unreliability they sometimes exhibit usually stems from their inability to commit to things. Their ability to adapt to changes of plans often means they will frequently cancel on you. This can be quite a problem between you and a Gemini friend if you like strict schedules set in stone. This fear of commitment can also make it difficult for Geminis to stick with their tasks and accomplish them before shifting their focus to something else. It's a form of impulsivity that differs from that of Aries, but it can lead to many of the same problematic outcomes, including rash purchases, getting into dangerous situations, and other unfortunate scenarios.

## Compatibility

Just as air feeds fire, so will Geminis find ways to have a meaningful bond with many fire signs. These relationships and bonds tend to be complementary, based on understanding and mutual completion. Being impulsive and energetic, an Aries will have a lot of understanding of Gemini's restless nature. Leo and Sagittarius, the other two fire signs, can sometimes be very compatible with Geminis, but it might take some work.

Gemini is highly compatible with air signs, especially Libra. Libra has a way of introducing balance into a Gemini's life. He or she will also bolster Gemini's own sociability, which can make life very fulfilling for Geminis because of the enjoyment they will get from meeting new people and learning new information. Plus, Gemini's love of conversation is another factor that makes them fit so well with the sociable Libra. Geminis also get along well with Aquarians, especially in conversations and the exchange of concepts since both signs enjoy intellectual stimulation. Things can also get rather interesting when a Gemini runs into another Gemini, particularly when both exhibit traits like curiosity.

Among water signs, all three might function with a Gemini, but they all possess certain traits that can easily become a source of problems. For instance, Cancers might disagree with a Gemini in marriage due to the latter's propensity to pay less attention to their home and instead seek outside socialization. Pisces too often have a rather private nature, which can easily come to blows with a Gemini's sociable attitude. Gemini's sociability also has the potential to provoke Scorpio's penchant for jealousy.

With earth signs, Geminis tend to have a lot of difficulty relating to them, but if enough lucky stars are aligned, and enough effort is exerted, Capricorn, Taurus, and Virgo can all function as a great stabilizing force in an otherwise hyperactive and hectic life of a Gemini.

## Love

Suppose you're trying to get into a relationship with a Gemini. In that case, you should know that they are curious, highly active, adventurous and will turn every relationship into a rollercoaster ride. Because of their variable and changeable nature, Geminis can also be very unpredictable, providing for many twists and turns early on and even later in a relationship. Of course, this can be fun and exciting, but it can also be a problem if the surprises that come your way turn out to be bad. Gemini's willingness to try new things and experiment generally makes them great lovers, which will play an important part in their romantic relationships.

Just like in other areas of life, though, problems will begin if Gemini gives into indecisiveness and fear of commitment. Therefore, it's important to tread lightly when getting into a relationship with a Gemini. You might find this difficult because they tend to be so exciting during the honeymoon phase, but you might end up with a broken heart if you aren't careful. One week you might find yourself having the best time of your life, but then suddenly, your world comes tumbling down the following week.

To avoid surprises, you need to be direct and communicate as much as possible with your Gemini partner. Their restlessness and excitement can make it difficult to know where you stand with the twins, so you might have to discover yourself by just raising the issue. Openness, sincerity, and ability to keep up intellectually, and fun-loving nature are the four best ingredients for a lasting, successful relationship with Gemini. If you prefer to stay home and aren't very spontaneous, though, it's probably not going to last. The twins can spend time looking for that special person who can keep up with their pace, but once they find them, they will unveil their committed, faithful, and deeply loving nature.

## Other Relationships

In friendship, Gemini adheres to quite a few of the same principles as in love. They require honesty, communication, and an ability to keep up the pace. Because of their sociability and craving for communication, Geminis need to stay in touch with their friends and hang out regularly. For Gemini, no truer words than "out of sight out of mind" have ever been spoken. It's possible for Geminis to have friends at a distance, but they will have to communicate all the time and with meaning.

Gemini's friends will also have to be outgoing and fun-loving. Just loving to have fun can be enough, though, as Gemini will have no problem organizing events and plan out your activities. From a non-Gemini perspective, the twins are some of the most fun people out there, so friendships with them are very eventful.

Despite their outgoing, restless nature, Geminis have a deep, sincere devotion to their family, but that devotion can sometimes fail to materialize through meaningful action. Sure, Gemini loves their family more than anything, but that doesn't mean they will always put family responsibilities first. They're not the best family member to ask to look after your dog or take it for a walk. Gemini probably will much rather leave that to you and go out instead.

As you can see, Gemini's nature and attitude make them very suitable for many work environments, but Gemini's potential indecisiveness and restlessness can be sources of annoyance for coworkers or supervisors. When they fall out of balance, Geminis will always want to jump from one project to the next, leaving many things only half-done. Therefore, they make a great pair or team with folks who can provide counterbalance and keep the twins' restlessness on a proverbial leash.

## Work

For Gemini, satisfying work is all about mental stimulation, which keeps them occupied and focused. Otherwise, Gemini is liable to get overtaken by their innate restlessness, and their level of concentration can suffer. Gemini loves to satisfy their curiosity, of course, so they enjoy all sorts of analyses. Another crucial aspect of Gemini's nature to consider when determining their perfect job is the sign's sociability. Gemini's cleverness and the ease with which they communicate will make them suitable for most jobs in today's corporate environment and beyond, but that doesn't mean they will enjoy all those positions.

Jobs that revolve around teaching and communication tend to be very enjoyable for Geminis. They will also enjoy working in a capacity that requires them to improve communication between others, such as by solving their disputes, for example. Gemini's restlessness and thirst for change and constant movement, physical or figurative, are not to be underestimated, though. If a job gets stale and ceases to stimulate Gemini's intellect, they will want to move on quickly.

Gemini's love for communication goes beyond just conversing with people. Many Geminis will enjoy working as translators, which can involve both direct and indirect assistance to other people's understanding. Most things that concern languages and linguistics will occupy Gemini's mind and ensure that they are both productive and fulfilled.

By extension, Geminis often find satisfying work in all manner of writing. Plays, novels, articles, or technical books - whatever it is, Geminis are likely to enjoy writing it. They will even find editing, proofreading, and other jobs that have to do with writing to be stimulating. Because of these inclinations, it's common for Geminis to end up publishing or owning or at least working at a bookstore. Geminis are generally good at multitasking, so their search for mental stimulation and fast-paced work can take them on many paths. Sometimes, Gemini won't be satisfied with choosing just one path and will instead turn their entire life into one big exercise in multitasking.

## Getting Along with a Gemini

The stuff we've discussed about Gemini's nature should already have given you a few ideas on how to get along with Geminis or at least how to maintain an already-existing relationship. A great way to get into Gemini's world is by sharing in fun times with them, which can happen by chance or by your initiative.

If you're setting up a date and trying to start a relationship with a Gemini, be spontaneous and mysterious. The fun-seeking Gemini will enjoy surprises, so you can always try to keep the details of a date hidden. Even if it's technically not the most exciting place or activity in the world, Gemini is likely to find the date more exciting because of the mystery. Making sure that it's an activity you yourself will have fun with is just as important because Gemini will feel the vibe of boredom if you aren't enjoying yourself.

Another approach is the intellectual route. If you are fairly intelligent, this will come naturally, but just starting a deep conversation about a painting or a philosophical topic can do the trick. The fun and the intellectual levels are the two main strategies to get close to a Gemini. To get along well as time progresses, you must get ready to deal with the quirks we've covered. If Gemini fails to adhere to the agreed plan or even stands you up, try not to take it to heart. If it happens once and is followed by a sincere apology, you can rest assured that it was just Gemini's restless nature and has nothing to do with you. If it happens more than once, though, then you should reconsider the relationship.

# Chapter Four: Cancer – The Crab

Cancer, also known by its astrological symbol as the crab, can perhaps best be summarized as the homemaker. While other signs like Aries and Gemini often find it difficult to stay in one place and focus on things for the long haul, the crab is the person who likes to grow roots. Cancer is a water sign with a cardinal modality, and it is ruled by the moon while being associated with the fourth house. The crab's season is in the period between June 21 and July 22, which means it corresponds to the start of the summer solstice in Earth's northern hemisphere. This season's relevance is in the copious energy that Cancer gets to absorb due to the abundance of sunlight and other life-sustaining resources. This influence works in unison with Cancer's cardinal modality, and the fact that the sign's date range begins with a new season.

Cancer has what could be described as an exclusive relationship with the moon. Much of our moons nature can be interpreted as symbolic of Cancer's key traits. Even today, the moon is viewed as a guide in many cultures because it lights our way at night. Just as a nurturing mother often breaks down food to make it more suitable for a child, so does our moon relay the sun's powerful rays to us.

Because of its many scars in the form of craters, the moon has frequently been perceived as a shield or protector of our planet. This influence gives Cancers strong parenting instincts, an urge to protect, and a deeply nurturing nature. Cancer's exalted planet is Jupiter, which infuses this sign with qualities such as mentorship. As a generally protective and maternal sign, Cancer can benefit greatly from an appropriate placement of Jupiter at birth.

## Personality Traits

As we just mentioned, Cancers are home-oriented, maternal, and protective. The natural and most comfortable state for Cancer is to have roots firmly in the ground and to be tied down by a plethora of responsibilities toward loved ones. Cancers enjoy being part of large families, including both extended family and their own immediate family. There are a few things in life that the crab will care more about than establishing and fostering harmony at home.

The fourth house is the house of home, and family influences Cancers a great deal. You will also often find Cancers maintaining traditional values and ascribing a lot of importance to historical continuity. Cancer is the person who cares about their family history and tries their best to cherish these memories. It isn't uncommon for Cancers to project this attitude beyond their family either. This means they are usually community-oriented and will enjoy participating and contributing to their wider community, although family takes priority over everything else. As such, the crab is often patriotic and feels very strongly about belonging to their community and serving the greater good. Cancers also have a long, strong memory and aren't afraid to show their emotional side.

As is often the case, when strengths go awry or are taken to an extreme, they can become weaknesses. With Cancers, one problem that might arise is an extreme attachment to things like belongings. This happens when a Cancer's homemaking instincts go too far, and they become obsessed with what they are building at home. Cancers can also become too needy and a project that state of mind onto others, overestimating just how much other people need them. Because of their long memory and a potentially obsessive nature, Cancers are prone to holding grudges, notoriously so. Overall, Cancers are also prone to all sorts of emotional vulnerabilities like shyness - and even reclusion. As such, they function best when they have at least one or two active, outgoing people in their life because these folks can be the crab's window into the world, so to speak.

## Compatibility

Cancers function best with other water signs and earth tones. With other water signs, Cancers enjoy a special understanding with them on a level beyond the conversation. This is because other water signs will either possess the same vulnerabilities and emotional depth or at least understand these crab traits. Two Cancers are usually a good combination in most kinds of relationships, including romance and marriage, where they can work together to build a wonderful home.

As for Pisces and Scorpio, both are highly compatible with Cancers, often in a complementary way. This means they usually have certain positive traits that Cancers lack, which can be highly beneficial in their lives. Pisces can introduce a Cancer to spirituality and philosophy in close or romantic relationships while a Scorpio can make them more passionate, sexually, and otherwise.

Because of the great compatibility between practical earth and emotive water, Cancers get along well with earth signs. Cancer's relations with Capricorns are a great example of the attraction of opposites. Being the crab's polar opposite, Capricorn can greatly benefit from a Cancer's caring, nurturing nature. But Capricorn's strong dedication to their work can function well with Cancer's homemaking skills to create a very strong family structure. When they pair up in a relationship like this, the sky is the limit.

Cancers also get along well with Taureans because of the latter's dependable, reliable nature, which the home-building crab will greatly appreciate. Virgo can also have a very positive influence on Cancer's life, especially regarding structure and joint effort.

The highly dynamic, changeable air signs can infuse Cancer's life with a level of excitement and freshness that Cancers will occasionally want or at least think they want. Once the relationship gets intimate and more serious, though, this can be the exact thing that annoys Cancers. Fire signs are perhaps the worst match for Cancers, with the most fundamental differences concerning lifestyle and priorities.

## Love

Being a home-oriented sign with strong protective and maternal instincts, not surprisingly, Cancers are among the most devoted and loyal partners in love. Emotionally and in every other way that matters, Cancer will be a very generous partner who keeps on giving. This can make Cancers vulnerable, but if they are balanced, most Cancers will make sure that they don't forget themselves and their own needs. Cancer will usually expect the same devotion and respect she or he gives to you. Something else that you can count on from Cancer is honesty and openness. These folks will tell their partner and clearly when something is bothering them.

Cancers want stability in their relationship, and they benefit from having a reliable partner whom they can count on. Cancers can get along well with outgoing signs in that they can split responsibilities between home and work and make an excellent team. However, Cancers still like a certain independence, despite their commitment to the home. With most Cancers, this need for independence is satisfied by having the occasional break that allows them to take time for themselves. They might like to spend this time withdrawn in their study, working on a piece of art, or reading something. They will thus recharge their batteries soon, and they will be back, giving their partner undivided attention.

One of the biggest problems with Cancers with love is their unwillingness to let go. When Cancer invests time and emotional effort into a relationship, they can become so attached to it and so unwilling to abandon it they will often stay in a relationship even when it gets toxic.

## Other Relationships

Cancers are folks who would take a bullet for their loved ones with no hesitation. Cancers enjoy spending quality time with their family, and they will never miss a chance to have a movie or game night with their loved ones. This goes to show that it's not just a question of duty or fulfilling some job - quite the contrary. It might be a duty to protect one's family, but it's a blessing that the crab truly enjoys.

The unfortunate thing is that even the most devoted and loyal Cancer can slip into the extremes we've mentioned, all while being unaware. Some Cancers are prone to mood swings or melancholic episodes, both of which can cause a lot of frustration for their family members. That's why it's important for Cancer to understand that their family members have their own needs of spending time alone. This simple truth can be difficult to accept for some Cancers when they give into neediness.

In terms of friendships, Cancers can be very sociable, but those chosen will usually be a select, limited group of people. Cancers don't see the value in maintaining an expansive network of acquaintances and shallow friendships, so they will prefer to build a small but very cohesive group they can be open and natural with. Friends of the crab should feel a fair bit special for making it through Cancer's many filters and getting close enough to enter their inner circle.

Cancers will maintain loyalty and devotion even after death has said its piece. These folks are nostalgic, traditionalist, and very dedicated to preserving memories. Old family albums and other stuff that keeps memories alive are important to Cancers, and they will keep them with utmost care.

## Work

Cancer's willingness to care for others and the sign's maternal instincts make them perfect for many jobs that entail caring for those in need, whatever that might be. Still, looking after other people is also part and parcel of some highly intense, dynamic jobs, in which case Cancer won't be thrilled. Cancers like to dispense their care in a way and setting that allows them to give individuals undivided attention, such as in therapy.

It's not that Cancers can't function under pressure - quite the contrary - but their homebuilding and nesting instincts make them more suitable for jobs in homey environments, so to speak. For all these reasons, Cancers are often found in many areas of the healthcare system. While enjoying slower-paced jobs, Cancers are vigilant and not prone to panic, so they can do rather well in healthcare jobs slow most of the time but with the potential to get hectic now and then, such as nursing.

As you can guess, Cancers love to work from home, and many will go to some length to secure a job that allows them to do this. Ideally, they will run their own business, especially one connected or physically adjacent to their home. On top of that, Cancers might enjoy managing places that provide temporary home or shelter, such as hotels, motels, various shelters, et cetera. As such, Cancers will extend their natural urge to accommodate others well beyond their family while still being home-oriented.

Cancers will often be found working as cooks or in some other capacity related to food preparation. Cancers usually enjoy working with children. They might do this as teachers, coaches, or with various jobs in orphanages. It's common for Cancers to get involved with various forms of social work too.

## Getting Along with a Cancer

As you can gather from what we've discussed thus far, Cancers can be difficult to connect with. They're not excited about meeting new people and expanding their circle of friends or even acquaintances, unlike other signs that live for socializing. Cancer will establish contact with people either if they *must* because of work and other circumstances or because they feel really drawn, which doesn't happen every day. That's not to say you can't talk to Cancers, of course, but if you are looking to get along with them and establish a more meaningful connection, it might take some doing.

Cancers are most likely to open up when they feel comfortable in a setting. The best way to approach them is in controlled conditions that involve smaller gatherings or on Cancer's own territory. The fewer people there are around, and the less hectic the situation, the more open Cancers will be to opening up to new people.

An important part of getting along with the crab is to have understanding and tolerance for their nature. Understand that Cancers can get morose or moody at times, usually for reasons known only to them, so you need to be the person who won't take their attitude to heart. In fact, Cancers can be prone to mood swings that not even they understand, so it's best to just roll with it and do your best to ignore the occasional negativity. Remember that Cancers require respect and gratitude when they earn them. They are devoted folks who will sacrifice a lot for the people they care about, but they will undoubtedly want to be acknowledged and appreciated for their efforts. It's important not to take your friendship with Cancer or their favors to you for granted.

# Chapter Five: Leo – The Lion

As the fifth sign of the zodiac and the rulers of the fifth house, lions are born between July 23 and August 22. This fixed fire sign is ruled by the sun, which ensures copious reserves of energy, drive, motivation, and ambition, all of which will often rub off on those around them. This is no surprise as the season of Leo more-or-less encapsulates the very height of summer. Leos are folks who generally enjoy being the center of attention, and they always do their best to make the best impression they can. Under their relationship with the sun, Leos themselves are proverbially radiant, at least with their confidence and pride. The sun's central position in our solar system is also symbolic of how Leo is often at the center of attention, community, or family.

Leo can come under the detrimental influence when Saturn enters the sign. Saturn rules Aquarius, the opposite of Leo, and it influences traits like restraint and wisdom. As such, Saturn will be a long way from home when it enters prideful, outgoing, and restless Leo. Therefore, folks who are born with Saturn in Leo must go the extra mile when trying to find balance in life. For them, it will be especially important to learn discipline, which can sometimes be taken too far into over-compensation. When that happens, Leo can become overly critical of themselves or too inhibited, both of which are contrary to the sign's true nature.

## Personality Traits

Leos are assertive and tend to be extroverted or at least highly capable and willing to interact with the outside world. Leo's fixed modality means that these folks are capable of great persistence and stubbornness, making them likely to commit to their efforts until the job is done.

Overall, Leo's personality's most positive and pronounced defining characteristics are confidence, courage, and boldness. Leos never seem to lack enthusiasm, not just for whatever they happen to be doing in each moment but also for life, in general. Leo can always reach within and find assurance in themselves where others might require support or reassurance from external sources. Not only that, but Leos are also often the folks who support, reassure, and encourage others. Besides being proud and having a strong sense of self-worth, Leos find worth in others. If you have a virtue you are neglecting or a talent you aren't developing, a Leo will be sure to point it out and help you make the most of your qualities.

Leos are also generous people who make good leaders in their own way. Leo might not be the person who organizes a team effort or manages the whole show, but they will do an excellent job of motivating and encouraging everyone in the room. What they lack in administrative skills, Leos will make up in their ability to inspire a crowd.

Leo's fixed modality and pride can lead to negative outcomes as well. Some Leos can be a bit too committed to a certain cause or idea, which can make them pursue it even when the rational part of their brain tells them to stop. When you add pride to this equation, it's easy to see how Leos can go astray, never admitting a mistake. Leos, with this flaw, can benefit greatly from learning to be better listeners.

As confident as he or she always appears, the lion can be insecure. Their love of the spotlight and the praise it can bring can turn into dependence on compliments and an obsession with other people's opinions. Leos will rarely show such insecurity, and those around them will be none the wiser, but they will suffer immensely if they go down this road. Leos, with this problem, can also get rather obsessive and jealous in romantic relationships.

## Compatibility

Leos naturally make for a good combination with most folks belonging to fire and air signs, while problems are more likely to arise with the other two groups. Being a fire sign, Leo is driven by the same boldness, impulsiveness, and assertiveness as Aries and Sagittarius, which makes them highly compatible. If you're a Leo running into another one of your kind, you will likely find common ground in creativity. One potential source of conflict between the two Leos is the sign's love of the spotlight. A Leo usually won't take kindly to another lion stealing their spotlight and pushing them to the margins. As such, interactions between Leos can give rise to great rivalries, which might not always be bad if the rivalry is healthy and productive. When taken to unhealthy extremes, though, rivalries tend to spiral into conflict.

Air signs tend to function well with Leo, just as air feeds the fire. The relation between Leo and air signs translates as the energy this sign can absorb from air signs to become stronger and overall better. As someone who likes the spotlight, Leo can benefit from Gemini and Libra's sociable and curious natures. Aquarius can do an excellent job of bringing more objectivity, thoughtfulness, and level-headedness to a lion's life. Like in a few other cases, the connection between Leo and Aquarius is often an attraction of opposites. When Aquarius thinks too much and gets lost in the woods of their own mind, Leo will pull them back out. When Leo gets too restless and carried away, Aquarius will remind them of the virtue of patience and objectivity.

Leos are generally likely to run into issues with water signs. The nurturing Cancer, for instance, can give Leo the care and the calm that the lion wants, but they will eventually disagree when Leo's outgoing nature conflicts with Cancer's preference to stay focused on the home. The situation won't differ greatly from Pisces and Scorpio, as both can enrich Leo's life, but disagreements are likely to arise. Scorpio's possessiveness is especially problematic, which can combine with Leo's jealousy into a rather problematic relationship. But Earth signs can give Leos the stability they need in life, but they are generally a poor match in intimate relationships. As co-workers, though, Leos can function rather well with earth signs, although Taurus' stubbornness can be a significant problem.

## Love

Leos are very expressive, and they tend to be direct, so you will usually know where you stand with them. If Leo has feelings for you, they'll let you know exactly what's going on, unless they're employing strategy. Leos are also very passionate in love, which is why relationships with them can be intense, especially during the proverbial honeymoon phase. Since Leo loves to share their enthusiasm and inspire the people around them, you can expect this is a major aspect of Leo's romance.

Don't let their excited, fun-loving demeanor fool you, though, as Leos will undoubtedly demand you to be fully committed and devoted. Leo enjoys attention, too, so their partner must be able and willing to provide it. Still, passion is one of the most important things in relationships as far as Leo is concerned, so their partners need to keep up, but Leo's energy and enthusiasm can get a little too intense, even for generally outgoing and energetic signs. So, if you ever end up in a relationship with Leo, you should also be able to assert your own wishes because your Leo might get caught up in their excitement and forget all about what you want and need.

It's not that Leo doesn't care about their partner, though. It's just that the lion can get a bit more self-involved than the average person, and it can be difficult for them to stay in touch with their lover's wishes if they aren't able to make these wishes known. Therefore, Leo's partner should be open and direct as it's the best way to avoid any misunderstandings.

## Other Relationships

Being a good friend of Leo's is something rather special, not because it's difficult to get close to them but because they are such a people magnet. The charismatic Leo will make friends wherever they go in life, so it's difficult to make your way through the crowd and become a close and indispensable friend of the lion. Leo is the opposite of Cancer. Leo likes as wide of a circle of friends as possible, which they get without making a conscious effort to build that circle. Leo's friends are also very diverse and can include all sorts of characters. The lion tends to be the center of attention in that circle. Leo is the life of the party, so many people they attract are just along for the ride because they like fun.

In a sea of acquaintances, Leo will generally know to appreciate those who are their real friends. Regardless of how many new acquaintances they make, at the end of the day, Leo will always be there for a friend in need because they are loyal and dependable.

Of course, Leo's character and likeability translate well into business relationships too. Leos bring energy, creativity, inspiration, and leadership to their workplace. Leos make solid supervisors, especially if they have the professional skills as well and understand the ins and outs of a project. With technical knowledge and their people skills, Leos can build very efficient teams and do a lot of big things. Still, the assertive and confident Leo can sometimes be misunderstood as bossy or egocentric, but this will rarely be the case once you get to know them.

## Work

Leo's love of attention and spotlight can already give you quite a few ideas about the jobs that they will enjoy. Since they are also creative, they do well as performers of all sorts, ranging from stand-up comedians to musicians to actors and other artists. Their colorful personality and confidence can sometimes combine with a knack for business, so Leos can end up as rather successful salespeople. Other jobs that rely on charm, character, and powers of persuasion are also generally well-suited for the lion.

For Leo, having their personality and character bogged down in a boring job where their qualities are buried under a strict, endless routine would be very difficult to live with. At the very least, Leo's job needs to be dynamic and stimulating, but the ideal is undoubtedly a career they are a center of. Leos make successful politicians and lawyers as well for obvious reasons. Both lines of work allow Leo to fulfill yet another one of their passions, which is to inspire folks. Some Leos will look for a career solely based on that, making them good inspirational speakers and many coaches.

Like Taureans, Leos enjoy luxuries and other finer things in life, all of which cost money. When Leo finds the perfect career and gets to work, though, he or she will have no problem making that money. Still, these material gains and comforts are merely a perk, and a lion would never be content with living in a cage, no matter how big of a salary he was offered. If a job is boring, and it doesn't allow their great character to shine and rub off on other people, it will be a dead-end job as far as Leo is concerned.

## Getting Along with a Leo

Almost everyone can get along with a Leo, but it's relating to a Leo that might be difficult for some signs. But Leos aren't complicated and generally very agreeable without too much effort. The first and foremost thing is to be *direct,* as we briefly mentioned above. The more honest and upfront you are about your wishes, intentions, concerns, or anything else on your mind, the better quality of communication you will have with Leo. Leos generally have little patience for subtlety, mind games, and ambiguousness.

What's also important is to just let Leo be what they really are. Leos are enthusiastic, fun-loving, and generous folks, so you need to allow them to be themselves in this regard. Try to avoid making it a big deal if they give you gifts, for instance. Instead, just roll with it and give Leo your thanks. Sometimes, Leo's friends must give them criticism or pull them back in some way, but do your best not to rain on Leo's parade unless you must. Leos expect their friends to partake in their fun and share their joy, so if your Leo friend isn't doing anything dangerous, don't shoot them down just because you don't find it fun.

Leos also like to be encouraged, appreciated, and to be told kind words. If you are someone important in Leo's life, remember that these folks care about approval and confirmation. When Leos are doing something, receiving encouragement and positive feedback from the people who matter can be a powerful boost.

# Chapter Six: Virgo – The Maiden

The Virgo season occupies a place after summer between August 23 and September 22. Ruling the sixth house, Virgo is ruled by Mercury and is an earth sign with mutable modality. Virgo is symbolized by the maiden or the virgin and has been observed and interpreted since ancient Babylon. In Babylon, the Virgo constellation was personified in the goddess Shala, the goddess of harvest and fertility, aspects of life which were of utmost importance to the Babylonians. This interpretation, especially regarding agriculture, continued to evolve along the same lines through ancient Greek and Roman societies.

Being a late-summer sign, the maiden occupies a period of decreasing warmth and daylight and shortening days. As the fall equinox approaches, a time of gathering and harvesting comes, which translates to Virgo's earthy nature and adeptness at the organization. Being the second mutable sign, born during a time of shifting seasons, Virgo is infused with adaptable and changeable energy and nature. The sign's earth element provides an influence that makes many Virgos highly efficient and industrious.

In Virgo, just like with Gemini, Mercury is an important influence that makes those born under the sign quick-witted and analytical. The maiden will likely come under the detrimental influence if Jupiter is in Virgo. Jupiter's influence is observed in Pisces, who is conditioned by this influence to be an explorer of great expanses. This energy will conflict with Virgo's penchant for strict and tight organization and their attention to detail. In practical terms, this placement has the potential to create a version of Virgo with the sign's traditional traits amplified into a negative extreme. Obsessive attention to detail and an extreme focus on control in every situation can be a few consequences.

## Personality Traits

Most of Virgo's qualities and traits can be classified as feminine, receptive, and yin, unlike Leo, for instance, whose traits are active, masculine, and yang. As such, Virgo is more oriented toward the inside, making those who are born under the sign more adept at introspection. Virgo possesses a deeper insight into their own inner world, blessing the sign with an elevated self-awareness.

Virgos are meticulous, adaptable, mentally agile, and usually have at least a couple of distinct skills. In Virgo, you will usually find a shrewd individual who is also a very quick learner. These folks are blessed with an observant and clear mind that allows them to think in objective, practical terms. Virgos also like to project this rationality and practicality onto the world as they enjoy bringing order to chaos. People under this sign love to improve themselves and everything and everyone around them, but they are also grounded, which protects them from the pitfalls of arrogance and self-importance. The maiden is also communicative and tends to be emotionally intelligent. This and their willingness to help is why Virgo is often the person who has valuable advice for others. Virgo will use their technical skills to help others in their physical endeavors as well as inner wisdom and awareness to give them emotional and other support.

One of Virgo's biggest problems is when their analytical, shrewd mind becomes too active. In extreme cases, some Virgos might collapse under the weight of their own thoughts, suffering from anxiety, excessive worry, and many a sleepless night. Virgo's natural inclination to serve and heal other people can also become extreme, leading maidens to neglect themselves completely and their own needs. Other extremes that Virgos can go to when they fall out of balance to include being overly critical of others or of themselves.

## Compatibility

Virgo is highly compatible with water and earth signs, while fire and air signs might require the maiden to put in extra effort if they are to function together in any capacity. Virgo is another practical, organized sign that can benefit from the healthy dose of vulnerability and emotional sophistication that water signs can bring to the table. Like with other signs, Cancer will treat Virgo with a lot of care, but Virgo can return the favor. Virgo's own nurturing and attentive traits will sometimes provide Cancer with some respite, which is a welcome change for Cancers since they do all the nurturing with most other signs. Virgo will also get along well with Pisces, with whom they will enjoy an attraction-of-positives relationship. The great polarization between the orderly, practical Virgo, and the philosophical, abstract Pisces can make for a wonderful complementary relationship when an understanding is reached. As is often the case, Scorpio can infuse this relationship with sexual magnetism, besides other interests that Virgo and Scorpio might have in common.

Among the earth signs, Capricorn and Taurus make excellent matches for Virgo simply because they have a lot in common, especially with their emphasis on stability, organization, and practicality. Capricorn and Virgo, both being natural perfectionists, can do incredible things when they put their two minds together. As we mentioned earlier, Taurus also brings a lot to the table for Virgo in the way of common interests, but one of the greatest strengths of these relationships is Virgo's ability to keep Taurus' indulgence under control. Two Virgos are also a great match in most contexts, including romantic relationships.

As before, this earth sign finds it very difficult to establish a meaningful relationship and mutual understanding with fire signs. Virgo shares its mutable modality with Sagittarius, which is some common ground that might lead to solid communication, but the natures and lifestyles of the two are so fundamentally different that it probably won't matter in the end. Air signs are neither here nor there since they can bring irreconcilable differences into the mix, but there is still potential for a complementary relationship. Ultimately, these are matched with the most variable outcomes.

## Love

Virgos are sensual, subtly passionate, and they don't shy away from commitment. Virgo's symbolism of the maiden or virgin symbolizes the way they are in love as well, to a great extent. Virgos are careful when embarking on a new romantic adventure, and they won't fall for someone so easily. They are very loving and devoted partners, but it might take time and effort to get them emotionally invested. Once Virgo has judged that someone is the right one for them, though, their love will open like a flower, and they will demonstrate immense devotion and faithfulness.

The introspective Virgo can appear uninterested and cold on the surface, but those who manage to get close to them will know that Virgo is incredibly passionate and can be very emotional. This hidden passion is like a buried treasure that will reward the person worthy of getting through to Virgo and becoming their romantic partner. On top of being passionate, Virgo is also helpful and supportive of their partner. Their stabilizing influence can do wonders to change someone for the better. It's common for Virgo to be that one partner who sets a person on the right path in life. Even if the relationship itself doesn't survive long-term, the positive influence will remain with Virgo's partner forever.

For Virgo, it's very important that they connect intellectually with their partner because they find the relationships predicated on an intellectual connection to be the most stimulating. Furthermore, Virgo is the person who selflessly focuses on learning as much about their partner as possible, including their interests, quirks, qualities, and other unique characteristics. In return, Virgo will expect or at least enjoy the same. Indeed, with Virgo, it's all about the little, personal things. Even an expensive present from their partner won't mean much to Virgo if it's thoughtless, automatic, pre-programmed, or a cliché. Virgo will be much happier if you give them a worthless, handmade gift, as long as it has your personal touch and symbolizes your understanding of Virgo's unique character and the connection you share.

## Other Relationships

With friendships, Virgo is a lot like the crab in the sense that their inward-oriented, reserved nature makes it a bit more difficult to get close to them. They won't be quite as careful as they are when picking a romantic partner, but they will definitely take time getting used to a person to a point where they can consider them a real friend and be comfortable around them.

Virgo is likely to be shy, but this doesn't mean they don't like to interact with people. But Virgos enjoy establishing a connection with someone new, but they don't always feel comfortable initiating contact. Depending on your character, you might have to break the ice and get Virgo talking. The best way to engage with them is through intellectual topics interesting enough to pique Virgo's curiosity. Once they open up and start talking about a topic that resonates with them, Virgos can open up a whole new, communicative side you didn't see before.

In professional relationships, Virgos are generally very good employees in most lines of work. Instead of talking too much or wasting their energy in some other way, Virgo will prefer to focus on their project and get the job done. This will score good points with many supervisors. They have analytical minds and a strong capacity for critical thought, so they are also good at solving the problems of other coworkers. If Virgo becomes too critical like they can at times, this can lead to issues both in the workplace and among friends. Therefore, some Virgos must go the extra mile to filter the things they say and keep their criticisms in the realm of well-intentioned advice.

## Work

As we already mentioned, Virgos are contemplative, reflective, analytical, and they have a sharp eye for all sorts of details. These qualities make Virgo great for certain jobs and determine which lines of work the maiden will find enjoyable. Virgo's earth element blesses the sign with stability and dependability, but the sign is also mutable, which means that they do need their job to be at least somewhat stimulating and dynamic. The schedule itself need not be dynamic, though. Virgo will operate best when their job gives them consistency and structure, and when their purpose is defined. The thing that will excite Virgo about their workplace is new projects that come as part of that job.

Virgos will be very useful in organizing a team or a workplace, even if they don't always feel like being the leader. As such, Virgo will do well as the person a supervisor might employ as a helper or consultant to tidy the place up. Virgos like clutter, neither physical nor any other kind, so they will enjoy putting things in order.

Virgos will also do an excellent job in any sort of data analysis or similar post where their analytical and meticulous mind can sift through information. Bookkeepers, accountants, analysts of different kinds, fact-checkers, editors, and other folks who must keep an eye out for the finer details are often Virgos. Folks born under Virgo do well with languages and literature, which is why they often make good writers, translators, and teachers. In general, Virgos are good at passing on the information and knowledge they have and explaining it to others. Besides teaching, Virgo can do well as a coach, tutor, or therapist.

## Getting Along with a Virgo

The first and perhaps worst mistake you can make with Virgo is to assume that they are cold and emotionless just because they aren't particularly expressive. As we discussed, Virgos are simply not very open and aren't eager to share their inner thoughts and feelings with just about anyone. The Virgo you've run into may be very emotional, but it will take time for you to uncover that side of their nature. So, you must remember to give Virgo space and show them you care about them through small but consistent actions that prove it.

Once you discover that Virgo is a generous person with a lot of understanding and forgiveness for others, it will be your responsibility not to take advantage of these things. Virgo will almost always give you the benefit of the doubt and a second chance, but instead of just apologizing and going back to whatever got you in the first place, you should strive to prove through action that Virgo was right to give you that benefit.

You must also remember how analytical Virgos are. They just love thinking and, occasionally, they will go into overthinking mode. If you aren't ready to deal with this, you will probably experience quite a bit of frustration when Virgo starts obsessing over something or getting anxious. They can work themselves up into quite a state and give into their insecurities. The least you can do is not make things worse by adding fuel to the fire. If you know how this particular Virgo can be calmed, though, try doing that.

Finally, be prepared for more criticism from your Virgo, no matter how close you are and how well you know each other. Virgos don't see this as a way of attacking you or hurting your feelings. They're simply analytical folks who like to keep things as perfect as possible, and they will analyze and comment on you as they would on anything or anyone else in life. When the criticism is valid and constructive, take what you can and move on. If not, just do your best to keep things cool and get both of you occupied with something else.

# Chapter Seven: Libra – The Scales

Libra, astrologically symbolized by the scales, has a date of the birth range that falls between September 23 and October 22. Libra is an air sign with cardinal modality and is ruled by Venus while occupying the seventh house. Libra's season starts just after the beginning of autumn in the northern hemisphere, right at the autumn equinox. The symbolic significance of the autumn equinox for Libra is in the fact this day will have equal daylight and darkness. This is in line with archetypical attributes of the scales, including equality, balance, justice, et cetera.

Being the third of the four signs with cardinal modality, Libra marks the beginning of autumn and is thus infused with initiative and leadership, like other signs that herald new seasons. Libra's air element is also very important because it's the source of their adaptability, sociability, and natural flow. Libra is a very active personality that has no reservations when establishing social contacts and exploring the world.

Venus, which is a force of peace, love, and diplomacy, can achieve its full potential in Libra. Therefore, not surprisingly, grace, elegance, and amiability are some of Libras' hallmarks. As for the planet that's exalted in Libra, that would be Saturn, the planet that bestows stoicism, wit, discipline, and a sense of duty. This is a very positive and fitting influence for Libra, whom Saturn can turn into an incredibly balanced and gracious individual that others will look up to. The peaceful and diplomatic Libra will come under the detrimental influence when Mars enters the sign, as can be expected. Those with Mars in Libra can end up a little too reluctant to confront and resist. Libra's seventh house, also known as the house of balance or sometimes the house of relationships, is another important influence in this sign. This is one of the main influences behind Libra's sociable nature and adeptness.

## Personality Traits

As you can probably gather, Libra is an outward-oriented sign that loves to engage with the world, explore, and especially to make contact and establish connections with the people they run into. Libras also excels at bringing people together, helping them overcome conflict, and just overall improving the cohesion of any team or community that the Libra finds themselves in.

As such, Libra is usually an excellent listener who not only sits quietly while others talk but truly understands what they are saying. Libras often put other people first, especially in the interest of a common good, so they have a great ability to empathize and to address people's grievances. Libra's ruling planet infuses this sign with love, balance, and healing, all of which the scales will project onto the world. Libra is also the kind of person who cares deeply about justice, both in everyday life and in the wider societal scope. In all, Libras are high relatable, agreeable, diplomatic, and easy to deal with because they always go the extra mile to sort things out between people. Libras are also often artistic or, at the very least, highly appreciative of art, thanks to their strong aesthetic sense.

Just like with other signs, many of the negative aspects of Libra's personality stem from their virtues, when these are taken too far or become warped. Libra's struggle is, in a way, the opposite of the struggle that some more confrontational signs like Aries must go through. Namely, Libras are often in danger of becoming too diplomatic and too wary of confrontation. Therefore, Libras can sometimes fall into the trap of passivity, at least regarding themselves and their interests.

Besides allowing others to walk all over them, these Libras will also be overly withdrawn and unwilling to share their true feelings. When they spend too much time bottling down these feelings, Libras can become unstable. Another problem that can arise with Libras is indecisiveness. Because Libras are so diplomatic and careful to consider every side of the argument or any other situation in life, it's easy for them to slip into a state where they spend way too much time analyzing instead of acting. One of the greatest Libra pitfalls, though, is the loss of self-worth. This is why Libras, especially children, should be reminded occasionally that they too are deserving of care, love, and understanding - all those things that the Libra gives to others.

## Compatibility

Libra's kindred spirits are usually found among other air signs as well as fire signs, while the other two groups can be fairly hit-or-miss. As usual, air will feed the fire, so the relationship with fire signs will mostly be complementary and very functional. Libras and Leos get along like peas and carrots due to their shared outgoing nature and Leo's passion. Because Libra is highly sociable, he or she will likely get along well with Sagittarius's adventurous disposition. The relationship between Libra and Aries will likely be an attraction of opposites where Libra will have a way of putting a lasso on Aries' hotheaded nature.

With air signs, Libras can greatly enrich the lives of Geminis and Aquarians. Aquarius is a natural conversational partner for Libra, as these two will have an endless stream of ideas and opinions to share and discuss. Aquarius sometimes lags behind Libra in certain areas, particularly romance and affection, so Libra might have to show patience in that regard occasionally. With other Libras, this sign can create a range of very interesting, usually highly functional relationships. The combined passion of two Libras can move mountains.

As usual, water signs provide emotional maturity and the vulnerability that some signs lack, which Libra can benefit from. Some traits that Libra has, however, are likely to eventually lead to issues. For instance, Cancer will have similar problems with Libra they would with Leo, mostly concerning Libra's sociability and outgoing attitude. The philosophical and emotional Pisces might end up frustrated by Libra's unwillingness to explore greater emotional depths instead of keeping things casual. As for Scorpio, they won't have much of anything in common with Libra. While Libra can garner some stabilizing influence from earth signs, these signs will ultimately remain a mystery for most scales. Short-lived relationships might be explosively enjoyable, but long-term prospects leave a lot to be desired. Outside of romantic relationships and serious friendships, though, Libras can get along with earth signs just fine, certainly enough to get a job done.

## Love

Libra doesn't like to be alone, so when they don't have a partner, they will seek one out. Libra might make this a conscious and active effort, or it can come naturally with little thinking. This sign's highly sociable nature allows them to make contacts wherever they go easily, and there's always a chance that some of those contacts will have romantic potential. Libra has a way of making their partner feel like the scales are just the perfect and ideal partner.

One way of putting it is to say that Libra loves to love. People born under this sign are the types who fall in love easily and intensely. Therefore, Libras generally have quite a few relationships, more than most other signs, before settling down with someone for good. However, once they do settle down, Libras will demonstrate that they are more than capable of long-term commitment. Libra's relationships will benefit from their ability and willingness to make peace and keep things in balance. Libras will naturally detect the traits in their partner they need to balance with, which is one of the main ways they make it work.

In general, Libras tend to be very attractive to others because they always have some quality about them that makes them very appealing. Whether it's good looks, clothing style, charm, or a combination of numerous factors, Libra usually has no problem attracting a potential partner. They are just very good at making people feel special, which they can do intentionally or instinctually. As much as Libras enjoy giving love, they do expect it in return too. Unless their partner makes an effort and commits, Libra's natural balancing abilities will probably not be enough, no matter how powerful they are.

## Other Relationships

Libra's balancing act plays an important role in their other relationships, especially friendships. Libras have a way of infusing their friends with feelings of strength and adequacy that can help them overcome their problems. As such, Libra will be a great source of encouragement and motivation for the people around them, especially the ones to which they are close. When a dear friend has an issue they are struggling with, Libra will take it personally and make it their mission to get their friend over that obstacle.

The outgoing and sociable Libra likes to have fun, so there's hardly ever a shortage of acquaintances end events in their lives. Libra's enjoyment of novelty and experimentation also makes them the kind of friend who will gladly go on all sorts of adventures. They are open-minded folks, which is a quality they can inspire in other, more inert folks, inspiring them to break out of their shell and explore new territories. Much of all, this applies to Libra's relationship with their family. Libra will be very devoted to their family and will often be the person who bridges the divide and sows peace and harmony among relatives and siblings.

Maintaining successful relationships in business and the work comes naturally to Libra. Sociability goes a long way toward making communication easier, but Libras also make good leaders, and their work can benefit from their creativity. As sociable as they are, though, Libras will often do well when assigned to specific projects they can work on alone. This in no way affects their ability to establish business relationships, however. In general, Libra's balancing powers and people skills can significantly improve workplace relations, including among other workers.

## Work

Working with other people, especially when helping them, is what Libras do best. Because of their relational skills and a strong sense of justice, Libras will shine in professions that revolve around helping the disadvantaged and unfortunate. Libra will enjoy fixing things for people, engaging in negotiations, and just making things better in general.

The stimulation and fulfillment that Libra seeks can hardly ever be found in jobs that entail too much stale routine or isolation from others. Libra needs to stay active and experience new things and challenges, so staying in one place for too long can wear this sign down.

Libra's keen sense of aesthetics, creativity, and desire to make everything more beautiful usually make this sign a good fit for all sorts of art disciplines. If a particular medium allows Libra to inspire others, create works of beauty, and express ideas, that art form will be fulfilling for them. In that regard, Libra might also be satisfied with similar work that might not be considered art per se, at least not in the traditional sense. Many Libras will enjoy working as interior designers, for example.

This sign's love of justice often leads them on a path to a law career, of course, so they might be found in courtrooms as lawyers or even judges. They might also end up being negotiators in different capacities, even in international diplomatic work. In these and other waters, Libras can also make good translators if they are born with a knack for languages. Making people's communication easier and better is something Libras can do in vastly different professions, including marriage counseling. The aforementioned factors combined make many Libras suitable for politics, so it's common for them to reach rather high in important leadership positions.

## Getting Along with a Libra

Being so outward-oriented and expressive with affection, Libra will respond well to the same treatment from you. This means that compliments can get you far with Libra. If they are good at something or if they're just wearing a very nice outfit, do your best to notice and compliment them on it.

Another great way to establish a connection with Libra early on is over something beautiful and highly aesthetic. For instance, visiting an art gallery, a museum, or anything else that entails beauty, especially artistic beauty, is a great idea for a first date with Libra. Better yet, if it's something that your Libra has never seen or experienced, this will be even better because they enjoy novelty so much.

You should let Libra take charge when they have to because their natural leadership affinities must come to the surface sooner or later. The best thing to do is to give Libra some support and subtle guidance. If they're leading on a project, for example, it's likely that they will come up with a bunch of strategies or approaches and have difficulty picking the right one. If you help them make that decision and stick with one approach, you will have provided exactly the grounding influence that Libra needs from you.

Overall, Libra might not respond well to harsh criticism, and they also don't like to confront people. You should avoid this approach when trying to get to the bottom of an issue or meaningfully converse with Libra. It's best to catch them in a good mood and be completely open and forthcoming about your wishes, concerns, and other things that you feel should be discussed.

# Chapter Eight: Scorpio – The Scorpion

Symbolized by the scorpion and originating from the Scorpius constellation, Scorpios are born between October 23 and November 21. This water sign has a fixed modality and is ruled by both Mars and Pluto, all while occupying the eighth house. As for symbolism, Scorpio's constellation has been observed and pondered over since ancient Babylon. This constellation includes a particular red star called Antares. In many traditions, this has been considered the so-called "heart of the scorpion" and a rival to Mars.

Scorpio's nature is further symbolized by the season that the sign occupies in the western tropical zodiac and the northern hemisphere, which is one where the sun's energy weakens, and darkness gains ground against the light. Just like this season, Scorpio can, at times, appear dark, shadowy, and above all mysterious. Not that Scorpios are always melancholic or morose like autumn, but they are largely inward-oriented, so they might give off that impression.

As always, modality and element are important influences that shape the nature of Scorpio. As the third of the four fixed signs that occupies a position in the middle of autumn, Scorpio is often the most fixed of all four. This is a source of many of Scorpio's strengths but also weaknesses. Scorpio's water element is usually the influence that balances its fixed modality and blesses the sign with creativity, an investigative mind, and intuition.

Scorpio is another sign with dual rulership. According to classical astrology, Mars rules Scorpio just like Aries, but it also has a modern ruler in Pluto. The reason this ruling planet is labeled as the modern ruler is that Pluto was discovered in 1930. In classical astrological tradition, Scorpio is the nocturnal domicile of Mars, while Aries is the diurnal one. This means that Mars' influence in Aries is pronounced, loud, and obvious to all, while in Scorpio, it's subtle and hidden, like second nature. Scorpio has the same capacity for aggression and strong ambition as Aries, but Scorpio will be much more calculated and reserved in how he or she uses these powers, being the proverbial dog that doesn't bark but can certainly bite. The co-ruling Pluto brings some of the themes and aspects characteristic of Scorpio's life, including deep introspection, destruction, and power.

## Personality Traits

Scorpios are curious individuals who love to investigate things and other people. They are the people who ask the real questions and have little use for pointless chatter and trivial questions that comprise little more than small talk. Somehow, Scorpio always gets right down to the gist of things and knows how to uncover all that is underlying. Besides their investigative and curious minds, Scorpios are also led by strong and accurate intuition.

Often, Scorpio will be a hard worker and a person with strong determination who knows devotion. Because of their diligence, hard work, creativity, and investigative minds, Scorpios are often found conducting research or undertaking various studies. The scorpion is the kind of person who takes a job and makes damn sure that the task is completed. Scorpios are also known for their patience and calculation in everything they do, especially when interacting with other people.

Scorpios can sometimes come across as edgy, shady, or cold, but this is just a natural façade resulting from their inward orientation and deep contemplation. As such, Scorpio can often be the proverbial outsider and someone whom others will consider to be peculiar. Scorpio is more than capable of establishing deep, meaningful bonds with others. Once someone enters their world and a bond is formed, Scorpio unveils limitless passion and devotion. While it can be difficult for you to earn a Scorpio's trust, it will become clear that the effort was worthwhile once you do.

One of the potential problems with Scorpios is the detriment of Venus, the goddess of love. When Venus enters this sign, Scorpio can be thrown way out of balance, especially in their capacity to love and connect with another person. Individuals with this placement have too much love and affection or too little of it, sometimes even coming into conflict with social norms in both cases.

Scorpios can also become problematic when their devotion and hard work turn into obsessions. These Scorpios are liable to become too rigid, and any meaningful change can be very difficult for them. The same can apply to Scorpio's (un)willingness to let new people into their life, as they can be notoriously slow to trust someone. Scorpios are also often the people who have a keen interest in all things dark, which, sometimes, can make them overly focus on this side of life, leading to all manner of dark thoughts.

The dark side of human nature and condition has a way of rubbing off on Scorpio, which can be a serious problem since many Scorpios find themselves right at home working with troubled people like counselors, social workers, et cetera. Scorpios thrive on understanding and support, especially from a young age. If you have a Scorpio child, for instance, it's important not to shame them when they express interests that are somewhat unconventional.

## Compatibility

Scorpio compatibility dictates this sign will operate best in the company of other water signs and earth signs. There is the potential for an explosive, passionate, and intense romance between two Scorpios, sexually and otherwise. Life can be quite an adventure when two Scorpios get together, especially when their urge to explore and demystify the world combines. Even when two Scorpios are too much alike and have flaws, they tend to understand and empathize with each other well. Scorpios also get along great with Cancers, mostly because they share the same sensitivities and comforts, particularly regarding privacy and home. Pisces is another sign that Scorpios will like to hunker down with. The two complement each other well and will often share a lot of the same interests.

Among earth signs, Capricorn is distinguished as a good coworker for Scorpio, and someone that Scorpio can have fun with during leisure. Capricorn's organizational skills and their ability to build will complement Scorpio's investigative and exploratory drive quite well on many projects. In romantic relationships, Virgo is usually a better match, making an excellent partner for the scorpion. Besides a high likelihood they will share interests, the two also get along well because they both have a longing for perfection in love. Taurus, the opposite, can be a source of great attraction for Scorpio. This match-up can be a great story of opposite attraction, but issues can arise if both give in to their natural unwillingness to compromise.

The volatility that comes with fire signs is something that most Scorpios won't appreciate too much since this is the opposite of Scorpio's subtle, private, restrained nature. Even though they are right next to each other in the zodiac, Sagittarius and Scorpio have virtually nothing in common. The relationships are akin to those with Aries, even though Mars rules Scorpio just like the ram. There is more common ground with Leos, but the two are still likely to eventually come into conflict when we take their jealousy, stubbornness, and passion into account.

When Scorpios become a little too accustomed to their solitary, withdrawn ways, running into a sociable and pepped up air sign can be a pleasant wave of refreshment. However, in the long term, the scorpion is likely to tire of these signs' changeability. Aquarius is a possible exception since there is some common ground with Scorpio, but the (potential) problem is this common ground largely revolves around the signs' stubbornness and love for debate.

## Love

As you can gather from what we've talked about, relationships with Scorpio can be intense sometimes. This intensity has the physical or sensual side because Scorpio is known for their passion and sexuality. They have a strong libido, partly because Scorpio's sexuality often serves as an emotional outlet. In all, Scorpio is hardly a simple sign, and it can be quite difficult to deal with for some signs.

Sexuality aside, Scorpios have simple and traditional attitudes toward relationships on the surface. They want real commitment and don't like to waste their time with pointless flings. They hate unclear, manipulative signals and the games that some people like to play in love even more. With Scorpio, it's all or nothing with no in-between. They expect you to be clear and upfront about your intentions, and they will let you know where you stand.

Psychologically intense and often subtly imposing, Scorpios can become rather controlling if their partner succumbs to their influence. Scorpio's partner should have a strong mind, character, and know-how to assert themselves. Partners who try to lie to Scorpio or manipulate them however, will usually have a bad time. Scorpio is intuitive for solving many problems, but he or she will also be very adept at detecting lies. Scorpio is probably way ahead of you when it comes to manipulation, so you shouldn't bother trying. That aside, Scorpio is a highly devoted, loyal, and monogamous lover.

## Other Relationships

A lot of what's true in romance goes for friendships, too, with Scorpio. Because Scorpio likes to be in control, their friends might sometimes find it difficult to assert themselves and their wishes. Scorpio can control things and pull strings so subtly, however, that you might not even notice when they're doing it. This is hardly ever because of some harmful intention and simply in Scorpio's nature. Just like in romance, Scorpio will be loyal and very devoted to their friends. The same holds true for Scorpio's relations with family.

With friendships, the main Scorpio problem is that they can be closed off and unwilling to let someone into their world. Scorpio's trust doesn't come easy, and it will be some time before they start talking about their innermost thoughts and feelings, if ever. Those Scorpios who give a little more into their dark, edgy nature can find it even more difficult to make friends because many people might feel uncomfortable around them or even afraid.

Scorpio's competitiveness and cunning make them naturally adept at navigating highly competitive business environments, climbing the corporate ladder, or outmaneuvering their competition. When they have a goal they are serious about,

Scorpios will do whatever it takes to accomplish it to the point of obsession. If they aren't raised with certain scruples and inhibitors, the competitive and cunning Scorpio can employ some shady, immoral means. Folks in a business relationship with Scorpio are well-advised to be careful and tread lightly, lest they get stung.

## Work

Scorpio's curious, investigative nature allows them to perform well in jobs where they are supposed to solve complicated problems or even mysteries, which hold certain answers that need to be uncovered. Scorpio loves the gratifying feeling they experience when they make discovery after a prolonged, intense investigative effort. Research, in the broadest sense, is where Scorpions can feel quite at home.

Investigative work that exists in private investigation, police crime investigation, or even intelligence services will suit Scorpio well. Not only do these jobs satisfy Scorpio's curious nature, but they can also provide a window into the darkness of humanity, which quite a few Scorpios will have a keen interest in, as we mentioned earlier. Scorpios don't mind dedicating years of their life to making just one discovery, so they can also make great scientists.

All of this is combined with Scorpio's subtle warrior nature brought on by the fact that the sign is Mars' nocturnal home. Therefore, it's common for Scorpios to be in the military and police in capacities other than just investigative ones. The dark side of Scorpio's nature can take them down many dark roads too, such as funeral work, the occult, or even various illicit activities.

## Getting Along with a Scorpio

It's important to be upfront and direct with Scorpio. This isn't just a matter of clarifying yourself and helping Scorpio to understand you better, though. Scorpios respect those folks who aren't afraid to stand up for themselves or even get into confrontations to get their way. That's not to say that you should be aggressive or purposely pick fights with Scorpio, of course. You should make sure that your wishes are known and that you're clear on what you're expecting from the scorpion.

Besides, honesty is simply a virtue that Scorpios hold in high regard. Remember that they are very intuitive folks whom some might even consider being walking lie detectors. If you try to lie or manipulate a Scorpio, they will be onto you quickly.

As imposing and strong as Scorpios appear they still need your support. In a relationship, it's crucial that you respect and foster your Scorpio's greatest strengths, such as ambition and persistence. If they're working hard on achieving a certain goal, give them all the support you can. Just don't forget about yourself and your own pursuits because if that happens, Scorpio might lose some of their respect for you.

# Chapter Nine: Sagittarius – The Archer

The archer symbolizes Sagittarius is its date range falls between November 22 and December 21 and occupies the ninth house. While its modality is mutable, Sagittarius' element is fire, and Jupiter rules the sign. Sagittarius is associated with the Sagittarius constellation, which was symbolic of the centaur Chiron in ancient Greek mythology. In Greek mythology, this half-man and half-horse called Chiron was the mentor of young Achilles long before he would have his legendary exploits. Chiron was a teacher of many disciplines, such as music, hunting, and medicine, while also being a prophet.

This ancient mythological account is symbolic of many traits we find in folks born under Sagittarius. Sagittarius is an adventurer, traveler, knowledge seeker, and generally someone who will go to great lengths in pursuit of underlying truths and wisdom. Chiron's kindness, generosity, and love of mankind are also reflected in most Sagittarians. A centaur's dual nature, being half-human and half-animal, is another characteristic that can be observed in most Sagittarians. This is because they possess a civilized, intelligent, and sensitive side while also having one wild, animalistic, and untamed.

The latter isn't negative since it symbolizes the free spirit and sense of adventure that Sagittarians have. The balanced Sagittarian is one that successfully maintains a combination of strong, clean instinct and deeper human wisdom.

The end of autumn and the onset of winter that come with Sagittarius's season both influence the sign. As a sign occupying a place at the end of a season, Sagittarius is the third of four mutable signs, which influences their changeability and adaptability. Sagittarius' fire element combines with their mutability, bringing energy, enthusiasm, and boldness to go along with the signs adaptable nature. This makes Sagittarius a natural explorer. Jupiter's influence is also important because it provides Sagittarius with the strength to persevere, giving this sign copious reserves of optimism.

## Personality Traits

Sagittarius is a freedom-loving wanderer, both literally and figuratively. Folks under this sign will love to physically roam and explore the world, but they also can't help but wander across the plains of all sorts of human abstraction, especially questions of life and meaning. Indeed, Sagittarius is deeply philosophical and is usually someone who is deeply concerned about things like the meaning of life, religion, and soul-searching. Sagittarians also are very introspective while also being very assertive and outwardly oriented.

Some of Sagittarius' greatest strengths include their boldness and optimism. They aren't afraid to take decisive steps forward while having faith in a positive outcome. This combination makes Sagittarians likely to succeed in the many endeavors that they undertake, whether professional, personal, or spiritual. On top of being adept at seeking the truth, Sagittarians are also good at sharing that insight since they make good teachers.

Even though Sagittarians can come across as restless because of their constant thirst for adventure, change, and travel, they are still governed by strong principles and are generally known for their integrity. Sagittarians will find it next to impossible to live under rules or adopt roles that conflict with their core values. When something does resonate with their values, though, Sagittarians are more than capable of committing themselves, especially when it's about a cause they deem worthy. Above all else, Sagittarians are distinguished by their honesty and sincerity.

This honesty, the defining characteristic it is, can be a source of problems, though. When they are thrown off balance, some Sagittarians can become too honest in a way that can be rather brutal. Furthermore, Sag's love of adventure and change is a rather obvious problem when it goes too far. Sagittarians can be notoriously unwilling to commit when you might want them to. They are also liable to change plans on people and shuffle their schedule around so it just doesn't work for most other people. Sagittarius' adventurism can also lead them way too far into fantasy land, and they will have to be restrained and grounded by well-meaning, realistic people. Therefore, it's important to teach Sagittarius children the value of discipline, structure, and organization.

## Compatibility

For the greatest compatibility, Sagittarius should look toward other fire signs and air signs. Two archers will get along well because they will understand each other's need for independence, exploration, and honesty. Aries is a great match for Sagittarius for similar reasons. Being a strong individual and a hard-charger himself, the ram can handle Sagittarius' brutally honest approach and their need for independence. Aries is the person who won't suffer and make things difficult for Sagittarius when the latter must spend some time away. This is precisely the potential source of problems with Leo, though, as this sign needs much more attention. Leo and Sagittarius can be a great match both in love and elsewhere in life absent this issue.

Libra and Aquarius can enrich Sagittarius's life by making the archer see more value in intellectual pursuits among the fire-stoking air signs. With their naturally curious personality, both these signs can go a long way with the adventurous and ever-inspired Sagittarius. Archers can also enjoy a deep, complementary relationship with Geminis. Like other air signs, Gemini brings curiosity, but this sign also has a playful or even mischievous side, which most Sagittarians will find highly stimulating.

Sagittarius can have significant issues connecting with water signs, though, and will often make these signs suffer. Many archers will find it difficult to appreciate Cancer's stay-at-home nature fully, and Cancers will usually find it difficult to deal with Sagittarius' constant craving for adventure. Pisces, too, will find it difficult to reconcile their need for privacy with Sagittarius' restless nature. Pisces can also be too sensitive sometimes, which doesn't mix well with the lack of filter that many Sagittarians are known for. As for Scorpio, this sign's propensity for jealousy will likely lead to many a fight with the archer. Earth signs often have the potential to restrain Sagittarius, but even they might feel it's a lost cause after a while.

## Love

The love of independence and novelty is what makes Sagittarians fairly difficult to deal with for some signs. Generally, the more a sign prefers predictability, stability, and routine, the more difficult they'll find it to function in a relationship with Sagittarius. Something else that can be a problem, especially for sensitive people, is Sagittarius' (in)famous honesty. Still, their honesty is likely to be a perk more than a problem usually especially with some signs that crave this honesty and upfront demeanor.

Being a fire sign that likes fun and leads a stimulating life, Sagittarius is very passionate. Emotionally, sexually, and in other ways, Sagittarius is the lover who will take their partner on adventures and into all sorts of new territories. Sagittarius lives to maintain their freedom and stay inspired, so a partner who can keep up with these basic Sagittarian needs can find a trusty and loving companion in Sagittarius.

Other Sagittarian traits, notably their emotional intelligence, can translate into great romantic successes. Sagittarius will understand their partner's ins and outs and, sometimes, they will know and understand their partner better than the partner understands themselves. Sagittarius will help their loved ones on their path to self-improvement and self-discovery, and they might be the decisive influence that sets someone on a new and worthy course in life. Sagittarius is also very trustworthy and generally the person in whom you can confide.

Even though a relationship with the independent-minded Sagittarius can appear scary at first it can be one of the most rewarding relationships you'll have. Sagittarius' honesty also reduces the risk of trying to be with them. Namely, the chances are small that you will get involved in a long-term mistake that will eventually ruin your life. Sagittarius will be honest and open about your incompatibility early on, so the relationship will be over well before things get too serious, if it was never meant to be.

## Other Relationships

In close friendships, Sagittarius will be someone you can trust and count on, but getting to that point is what's usually difficult. It's not a matter of Sagittarius' reluctance or introversion like with Scorpio, though. With Sagittarius, the issue is that they are constantly on the move and looking for new excitement. It's common for Sagittarians to maintain their friendships on and off, so to speak. No matter how close you are to Sagittarius, it's possible that they'll drift away at some point, but they will have no problem popping up again and getting right back into your life later. With signs that are independent and restless like Sagittarius, this isn't a problem, but the more attached and sensitive folks will probably have a problem with Sagittarius' ways. One thing is for sure, though: If you call when in need, Sagittarius will come. The archer is very similar in family life.

In the workplace, Sagittarians get along best with folks looking to work with flexible, creative, and innovative people. The problems start when Sagittarius is expected to uphold a schedule and rigid routine. As soon as they feel trapped, they will buck. Worse yet, the prospect of blind obedience to authority is horrifying to most Sagittarians, so they can be a big problem for supervisors who fail to understand the archer's nature. Given just enough freedom and space while being reminded of their job, Sagittarians can be excellent subordinates, but they need your respect. The Sagittarius' need for independence shouldn't be a problem. It's through that independence that their qualities like innovation and unconventional thinking can shine and produce great results. Harnessing a Sagittarius' nature in the workplace will probably pay off for everyone in the end.

## Work

The things we've just discussed will determine which jobs are suitable for Sagittarius. One thing bound to motivate and stimulate Sagittarius is a sense of belonging to something greater and especially serving a higher purpose. A stimulating, dynamic job that brings novelty and harnesses the archer's adaptable nature, all while providing a sense of great purpose in the big picture, will probably be Sagittarius' dream job. Due to their fiery element and nature, archers also enjoy a challenge, so they are unlikely to prefer some job based on how easy it is. Often, the difficulty is not really a factor for Sagittarius.

Based on all this, you can see how Sagittarius might find a fulfilling calling in some form of activism. Activism gives archers a purpose and challenges them, but it also relies on the innate optimism that Sagittarius draws from Jupiter. Sagittarians also tend to enjoy teaching, although the subjects that they will be interested in can vary from one individual to another. Because of Sagittarius' tendency to be empathetic and their activist inclinations, they can often be found volunteering in different capacities. In fact, archers might dedicate their entire lives to selfless work for the disadvantaged, suffering folks without asking much of anything in return.

Any job that entails physical travel is likely to appeal to Sagittarius. You can also consider how that might combine with the preferences we've discussed above. Sagittarius can often be the kind of person who organizes humanitarian and relief efforts or participates in them, regardless of where in the world that path might lead.

## Getting Along with a Sagittarius

As you can see, if you love adventure, change, and don't mind giving people the independence and the space they require, you have a strong basis to get along with Sagittarius well. Unfortunately, many folks will find it difficult to deal with the archer's restlessness and thirst for change. When a Sagittarius gets bored with their life situation, their romantic partner or friend might take it personally if they don't understand Sag's nature. This can lead to insecurity and a plethora of problems that stem from that. It's unfortunate because Sagittarius' restlessness isn't something anyone should take personally - it's just the way they are.

One of the most important prerequisites to get along with Sagittarius is to come to terms with their thirst for change and just accept it. Do your best to keep up, not just because it will maintain your relationship but also because you yourself might have a lot of fun and learning things you never knew about yourself. However, if you eventually tire of your archer's constant adventurism, then you should tell them. This is the second most important thing - be open and upfront. Remember that Sagittarians are also empathetic and have a lot of understanding for people. If they care about you, they will understand that they need to slow things down, which they will do for the right person.

Finally, prepare for a lot of honesty on a level you might not be used to. Sagittarians might openly tell you things that others would never dare, and they probably won't even stop to think about whether they are appropriate or not. Getting along with Sagittarius will require some thick skin. Besides, growing a thicker skin will help you in life, regardless of your relationship with the archer. It's just one of those things that your Sagittarian friend or partner will give you as a gift, which you'll continue carrying even if they eventually leave your life.

# Chapter Ten: Capricorn – The Sea-Goat

Capricorns are born between December 21 and January 20, making them the last of the four cardinal signs whose element is earth. Capricorn stems from the constellation known as Capricornus, also known as the horned goat. Capricorn is symbolized by the sea goat, which is a mythological, aquatic creature that is half-goat, half-fish. Capricorn also occupies its corresponding tenth house and is ruled by Saturn.

The legendary sea goat's mythology goes back to at least the Bronze Age, and different cultures have given different accounts. In ancient Babylon, the sea-goat was treated as an aquatic god associated with knowledge and creation. According to Greeks, however, there was Pricus, a sort of progenitor of a whole race of sea-goats. Pricus was father to many sea-goats he tried to protect, and the story goes that Pricus failed to protect his children and was given a place to live in the sky after this great loss. That place, the Greeks believed, was the Capricornus constellation.

Mythology aside, an important influence on Capricorn is the winter solstice that begins in the northern hemisphere with the start of this sign's season. During this time, the sun provides the least amount of light and heat. Capricorns are resourceful, and they always have a plan, just like winter has always dictated to all who wish to get through it. Being the last of the cardinal signs and heralding the beginning of winter, Capricorn is infused with the same initiatory qualities as the other season-starting signs. Capricorn's earth element's nature is also quite clear in many of this stable and level-headed sign's traits.

When Saturn is in Capricorn, the planet is in its nocturnal domicile, the diurnal one being Aquarius. Saturn in Capricorn gifts those born under the sign with ambition, discipline, practicality, productivity, and organization. Capricorn is also a sign where Mars is exalted, putting many of the sign's strengths into overdrive and making Capricorns extraordinary individuals.

## Personality Traits

Capricorns generally distinguish themselves as hard workers and folks who are goal-oriented, driven, and industrious. Capricorn is at their best when setting an ambitious goal, charting a path, and getting to work toward accomplishing that goal. They are very adept at creating projects and seeing them through, so they have a mind that's just right for business. Even when it's not about business, Capricorn will apply a business mindset to many situations in life, and it will often work out just as they had planned.

On top of their practicality, Capricorns possess patience and a high degree of realism in their thinking. When the going gets tough, and most other people are ready to throw in the towel, Capricorns will stay the course and keep grinding until the goal is achieved, and then they will relish in their glorious success. Capricorns are also usually good at giving advice to others, thanks to their own stability, level-headedness, and self-mastery. Sea-goats aren't committed just to their earthly pursuits and business ventures but also to the people they care about. They're not always as quick to trust as many would like them to be, but once they've established a connection, Capricorns will be the picture of loyalty. Capricorns are also known to have a strong sense of humor that serves not just to make people laugh but also to get the sea goat and those around them through hard times. It's that sense of humor that's often the ace up Capricorn's sleeve and the secret to their awe-inspiring perseverance and resilience.

As you can probably imagine, one common issue that arises with Capricorns is when their focus on the goal transcends the realm of rational. Indeed, Capricorn can get so intensely focused on their goal they become blind to everything else. This level of stubbornness can be rather destructive to Capricorn and even the people around them, particularly regarding their relationships. Because of their incredible work ethic and diligence, some Capricorns might hold other people to an high standard. There is nothing wrong with expecting people to do their best, but when Capricorns take this to an extreme, they can be difficult to work with.

One of the darker roads that Capricorns might get on is the road to isolation and solitude. When they are insecure or get disappointed, they might turn completely to their self-reliant nature and shut the whole world out. Many Capricorns will also hide their true feelings, especially pain, behind a veil of humor and self-sufficient attitude. When this Capricorn's friends don't understand them, their life's experience can become very lonely and isolated, even around people.

## Compatibility

The signs that can look forward to the best relationships with Capricorns are water and earth signs. Being a realistic, grounded, authoritative person, Capricorn will likely run into quite a few issues with fire and air signs. Those pesky adventurers and dreamers will often have to be talked down and restrained by Capricorns.

In all their objectivity and authority, Capricorns can sometimes forget their emotional side, which is why water signs can be so good for them. Cancer and Capricorn, for instance, can function well as a pair despite being opposites. While Capricorns can turn into workaholics, Cancers will focus on maintaining the home front. When these two reach a mutually-acceptable agreement and divvy up their responsibilities this way, they can have a very productive relationship, especially in marriage. If Capricorn can overlook Pisces' lackluster organizational efforts, he or she might benefit greatly from Pisces' ideas, which can broaden this sign's horizons. Capricorn also gets along well with Scorpio and is one of the few signs to have that ability.

As you can imagine, Capricorns are right at home with other earth signs because of their stability, order, and practical nature. When two Capricorns get together, no goal is too high or too ambitious. Because of their strong focus on work, two Capricorns may forget all about romance, so perhaps the best relationship for these two is close professional collaboration. Virgo and Taurus are also highly compatible with Capricorns, but these two have more to offer in the way of fun, leisure, enjoyment, and just all those nicer things in life, so they can both complement the hard-working Capricorn well.

Among fire signs, Aries is problematic for Capricorn because the ram is a headstrong individual with a penchant for leadership, which can easily lead to conflict with the authoritative Capricorn if both are uncompromising. Sagittarius is an even worse match-up due to several fundamental differences in values and in the way these two perceive the world. The situation is largely the same as Leo. These signs might function with Capricorn in some context, especially in business, but their long-term prospects for closeness are slim. Air signs can be even better for Capricorn when it comes to business, but long-term commitments will still often turn sour.

## Love

The sea goat, being an authoritative and hard-working individual, will require a lot of the same from someone they would consider a worthy partner. Capricorn will prefer to be with someone whom they can respect, depending on how many qualities that they respect can be found in that person. Capricorn will thus probably be the happiest in a relationship of true equals. Even though they are authoritative often and interactions in life, most Capricorns aren't looking for someone who will just submit to their whim with love. On the flip side, they aren't looking for someone who will dominate them either, but they are likely to have more respect for that person, at least.

Capricorn in love can perhaps be best described as they would be in other walks of life - a hard worker. This means they can be devoted, loyal, and committed, but they might not show it emotionally. You have learned that many Capricorns won't show many emotions, and the same applies to romantic relationships. If you aren't particularly needy or too dependent on romance, this won't be a problem for you. If you're looking for a partner who is strong, loyal, and protective, then the sea got will be worth the effort.

Besides, even the least expressive among them are likely to open up emotionally at some point, even if it takes years. This is because Capricorns view relationships just like they view their work or any other effort in their life. They employ a practical approach, and they get to work, expecting this will yield results. It's a simple concept, yet some of the more sensitive and emotional signs will have a very difficult time accepting it.

## Other Relationships

With friendships, Capricorns are all about quality over quantity. They will usually have only a few friends, but these will be true, long-standing friendships that might go as far back as childhood. These are relationships that Capricorns will work hard to maintain, and they will be very loyal to these people. The sea-goat will still rarely be all that warm and fuzzy with their friends, as close and trusting as they are for each other. One of the strongest foundations for friendships as far as Capricorn is concerned is intellectual connection.

Capricorns are tirelessly devoted to their family. The one thing they can get somewhat sentimental about is family memories, traditions, and wider history. The sea goat is usually well informed on their family history, and they feel a connection to that long-standing continuity. Somewhat surprisingly, Capricorns ascribe more importance to things like birthdays, anniversaries, family gatherings, customs, and other traditions. The one thing that Capricorns can't stand is nosiness and attempts at control, whether they come from family or friends.

The sea goat carries many of these principles over into their professional life. They are polite, professional, and well-mannered, but they also have a no-nonsense approach most of the time. If you want your Capricorn coworker to have a leisurely chat with you, then you better make sure that the topic you have to offer is interesting and intellectually stimulating. Otherwise, your Capricorn colleague would rather just go back to work. Capricorns are loyal, reliable coworkers who tend to exert authority even when they aren't in an authority position on paper. They are the person who always seems to have their stuff together better than other employees and is the one whom everyone asks for advice and assistance.

## Work

Capricorns are most comfortable when they oversee their work, which means organizing their time, environment, details of the project, and other stuff that goes into an assignment. This means they have no problem getting the job done when told to by their superiors, but best to let Capricorn retain a degree of independence because they will usually come up with the best approach to do the job right.

Capricorns can fit in and function in most workplaces and on a wide range of jobs. They are diligent, detail-oriented, well-organized, meticulous, and perseverant. These things make them great workers, but they also give Capricorn an edge in business when they go in for themselves. Capricorn will be very happy when they are their own boss, and they are successful as such.

Even though they prefer to work alone and focus on long-term projects, Capricorns can also treat people like projects. This makes them adept at human resources management. With their hard work, Capricorns can patiently work with people to get them on the right path, and with their eye for detail, they will usually sniff out the hidden potential in employees. Capricorns will do fine in all sorts of other managerial positions. As you can see, it's not just about sheer authority, of which Capricorns have plenty. Capricorns simply have a range of qualities and strengths that naturally project authority and inspire confidence in others making no conscious effort to do so. This makes Capricorns excel at most jobs they might take.

## Getting Along with a Capricorn

To get along with Capricorns, you must first learn not to mistake their default friendliness and courtesy with closeness. If you spend enough time with a Capricorn whom you've just met, you will quickly realize that despite their friendly and respectful demeanor, there is an undeniable distance that's always being maintained.

One possible way of catching a Capricorn off guard and getting close to them is by inspiring them to have fun. The hard-working, highly practical Capricorn can often forget to have fun and just unwind occasionally. If you convince them to take a bit of time to relax and introduce them to some fun activities they end up enjoying, this can be a strong foundation for a more meaningful bond. It's a way of catching Capricorn by surprise and leaving a positive impression. For Capricorn, it's not every day that someone swoops in and shows them aside from that they didn't know they had because the sea-goat usually has a very strong command over themselves.

Capricorns also enjoy accepting a challenge and learning new things. A good way to get closer to a sea-goat is to take them along for some meaningful activity challenging and stimulates them with new knowledge or skills. Taking up a new hobby, sport, or outdoor activity can be just the thing to make Capricorn want to spend more time with you. Other than that, just remember those things that Capricorns respect, including hard work and stability. Just having a sufficient level of understanding for Capricorn's nature will be enough to keep you two on good terms, at the very least, at the workplace or elsewhere.

# Chapter Eleven: Aquarius – The Water Bearer

The eleventh sign, occupying the corresponding house, is Aquarius. This sign's season is between January 21 and February 18. Aquarius is also known as and symbolized by the water bearer, and it is a fixed air sign. Saturn rules Aquarius, but, like Scorpio, Aquarius also has a modern ruler, which, is Uranus. This sign stems from the Aquarius constellation, which is symbolized by the water bearer or the mythological Ganymede, according to ancient Greeks. Ganymede was the son of the Trojan king, Tros, who eventually served as the cupbearer of the Greek gods on Mount Olympus.

In ancient Babylon, Aquarius was associated with Ea, a god known for carrying a vase full of water. Ancient Egyptians, too, had their own ideas about Aquarius, strongly associating it with the life-sustaining floods with which the Nile irrigated their crops. Egyptians believed that the flooding came when Aquarius would put his jar into the Nile.

As a fixed sign, Aquarius is under influences that give this sign stability and strength to endure. This is exacerbated by the signs positioning in winter, which is also the reason many Aquarians find themselves to be more creative and productive during the colder time of the year. As we mentioned earlier, Aquarius is the diurnal (daytime) domicile of Saturn. This allows all of Saturn's qualities to come to light and be at their best. With Saturn in Aries, folks are intellectually gifted and well-suited for a wide range of intellectual tasks while also being gifted with endurance, objectivity, patience, and other qualities. But Uranus infuses Aquarius with inventiveness, adaptability, and a penchant for unconventional thought and action.

Aquarius can give some disadvantages to those born under it if the sun enters the sign. The sun is in detriment in this sign because its home, Leo, is the opposite. Sun's radiance and imposing nature are quite the opposite of most Aquarians. Whereas Leos love the attention, Aquarians prefer to stay subtle, and when the sun is in the sign, Aquarians can shy away from attention to the point of letting opportunities pass them by.

## Personality Traits

Aquarians are often humanitarians and philanthropic individuals because they like to keep their eye on the big picture, and, as a result, they tend to care about making the world better. Aquarians usually have a keen ability to think ahead, and they are often proponents of progressive ideas both in personal life and regarding society. Aquarius won't shy away from establishing contact with folks who will help them on their mission, so they are often fairly well adept at collaboration and team efforts.

Even though it might not appear that way, Aquarians are outward-oriented signs who actively engage with the world. They are more than willing to commit, and they are the people who see their projects through. Aquarians are also very principled, and they adhere to their set of values, especially in social interactions.

Aquarius' greatest strength is probably their intelligence, which Aquarians combine with great objectivity. Aquarians are very good at observing things from a neutral standpoint and passing rational, objective judgment on situations and people's character. Even though Aquarians are usually functional, many will feel like they don't belong in much of mainstream society. This is something they feel on the inside, usually because they are full of novel ideas, but it rarely impedes their ability to function in society.

It's Aquarius' intelligence that can eventually cause problems for them, particularly if they become too intellectual at the complete detriment to all other ways of perceiving the world. Overly intellectual Aquarians can come across as cold and distant, and they might forget to give their loved ones the attention and emotional support they need. When Aquarians like these encounter situations that require intuition or emotional intelligence, the water bearer might become stuck and unable to find the solution. Aquarians can become way too fixed because of their rigidly logical approach and modality, especially when demanding certain standards from other people.

## Compatibility

Aquarius can get along well with fire signs and other air signs while the other two groups may or may not be suitable, depending on the context. Since Aquarius can come across as distant Sagittarius and Aries will bode well because they, too, are individualistic and won't require copious amounts of attention. The adventurous Sagittarius will appreciate Aquarius' unconventional behavior and approach since this is an affinity that both signs possess. Aquarius and Leo can make a great couple in a rather complementary relationship, particularly with Leos, who get out of hand and could benefit from a voice of reason that Aquarius will bring.

As for air signs, the intellectual attraction and the great back-and-forth that it can produce between Aquarius and Gemini will sometimes turn out to be just that - an intellectual connection. These two can thus be great coworkers or friends, but romance might not be the biggest priority often. Intellectually, Aquarians will also have a lot to share with Libras, but the relationship might eventually turn cold if Aquarius grows distant and forgets to give Libra the romantic attention he or she needs. Still, Aquarius might feel the most understood and comfortable when running into another Aquarian, especially regarding the exchange of ideas, communication, and mutual understanding.

When Aquarians get too immersed or even lost in their intellectual and abstract world of ideas, they can often neglect the emotional side of things. Water signs can come in with a lot of positive influence when that happens. Unfortunately, that's precisely what can lead to problems with these signs. It's not just that Aquarius doesn't care much for romance or emotional expression - sometimes, they quite literally can't handle intense emotional displays and requirements from others. Pisces' sensitivity, Cancer's attachment, and Scorpio's jealousy can all be the thing that eventually pushes Aquarius away. Earth signs are even less relatable for Aquarius.

## Love

With romantic relationships, the thing that can pique Aquarius' interest in something more than anything else in the world is intellectual stimulation. Many things that other signs care about will be very uninteresting for Aquarius, but if someone has something clever and interesting to say to get an Aquarian's mind gears going, then they will have Aquarius' attention. Under this sign, folks are all about having long, intelligent conversations about a wide range of important, deep topics.

After Aquarius has been wooed with cleverness, though, they will require more than an intellectual connection to keep a relationship going. Aquarians value honesty, and independence. They enjoy getting caught up in their inner contemplations from time to time, and so they will go on something of a loner streak at times. Simply put, Aquarius wants a certain degree of space, which they will also grant to their partner.

Aquarians usually prefer to be in a relationship with someone largely on an equal footing with them, just like Capricorn. But Aquarians are also known to make very unconventional choices when picking a partner. At any rate, once they pick a partner and the relationship gets underway, the commitment is for the long term. One thing to remember about Aquarius is that they have a very unforgiving nature. It's best to discuss any grievances and other issues ahead of time than to cross an Aquarian or mess up in some way. Once they feel betrayed or seriously wronged, it's probably over.

## Other Relationships

It's common for Aquarians to have a wide circle of friends and acquaintances, but they will only consider a select few to be their true friends. With those folks, Aquarius is very devoted and loyal. They prefer to be close with clever, creative, and honest people, as these three things are undoubtedly the strongest foundation for long-term friendship for Aquarius.

Aquarians have many friends because they are likable and easy to get along with on a superficial level. A wide circle of friends is more a natural, spontaneous thing than something that Aquarius strives for. Most Aquarians don't need many people in their life at all - it just often happens that way. They won't really open up to most of these people or let them into their life in some meaningful way because Aquarians like to avoid being emotionally vulnerable wherever possible.

However, with their inner circle of friends and family, Aquarians are open and will sacrifice a whole lot for their well-being. They'll also have a significant interest in sharing and discussing their feelings. Even though they like some alone time and will take a while to open up, Aquarians are nothing like Capricorns, for example. This makes it easy for Aquarians to fit in at their workplace and get along with coworkers. Because of their wit and diligence, they're good workers from a supervisor's perspective.

## Work

If a job allows Aquarius to use their individual talents and employ their intellectual prowess, then they will probably enjoy the work. Aquarians will be the most productive when they are in a workplace that fosters and encourages their creativity, imagination, and ability to think outside of the box. Indeed, Aquarius will often think unconventionally, which can lead to quite a few interesting ideas that can produce great results if they fall on the ears of receptive folks or if the Aquarian has the resources and the time to implement the idea on their own.

Since Aquarians like to be intellectually stimulated, they feel right at home in positions where they get to learn a lot of things. Aquarians are often scientists and researchers of all sorts. These jobs can also satisfy another passion that Aquarius has, which is their humanitarianism and a strong drive to make a positive change in the world.

This can translate to social work and other similar callings. All Aquarians like intellectual stimulation, but their interests will vary, and that stimulus can come from different sources. Whereas one Aquarian might find this thrill in science, another might have an interest in people and their troubles, leading them to become a therapist, counselor, or something similar. Aquarians can make excellent team players too, but they need to be assured that their contribution will be acknowledged when the job is done instead of being diluted with the rest of the team.

## Getting Along with an Aquarius

As we already mentioned, Aquarians love to be intellectually stimulated, so this is always a great path of approach to get closer to them and establish a connection. The challenging part might be to approach them or start an interaction, but once you get to a certain topic that can spawn a long and thought-provoking conversation, things will click on their own.

Keeping a meaningful conversation going will get you closer to Aquarius' heart. If you win a debate, present a strong argument, or otherwise get your Aquarian to think in a new way or see a fresh perspective, then all the doors will open. As someone who loves to think and contemplate, Aquarius will be excited to learn about something new or see one of their old arguments in a new light. They will immediately develop a great liking for the person who made that happen.

Remember that Aquarius values their independence and space, so be prepared to grant them that. This part is important because of you as well since some folks will often interpret Aquarius' occasional distance as coldness or anger. It's not something you should take personally and should just learn to live with. Something else you'll probably have to live with is all sorts of quirks that individual Aquarians might have. Often, these quirks are just something that makes them special and likable.

# Chapter Twelve: Pisces – The Fish

The twelfth and final sign of the zodiac is Pisces, born between February 19 and March 20, residing in the twelfth house. This is a mutable water sign that is ruled by Jupiter while also having a modern ruler in Neptune. The Pisces constellation has been observed for a long time and connected to many gods and godlike entities by various cultures throughout history. The sign's name comes from the Latin word for fish. Some of Pisces' associations include Poseidon or Neptune, Vishnu, some Sumerian gods, and even Jesus Christ. The ancient Greeks saw Pisces as the heavenly incarnation of the legendary fish credited with saving Aphrodite and her child from Typhon, a sea monster. The fish's distinguished place in the heavens was a divine reward for this action.

Since the western tropical zodiac puts Pisces at the last part of winter in the northern hemisphere, Pisces witnesses a gradual return of warmth and growth of daylight as spring draws near. It is a time that heralds an incoming season of renewal, growth, and awakening, which is reflected in Pisces in numerous ways. Pisces also draws important influence from its position as the last of the four mutable signs, making Pisces very capable of change and adaptation. This adaptability and capacity for change are further bolstered by the sign's water element.

While Jupiter finds its diurnal domicile in Sagittarius, Pisces is where the mighty planet rests at night. The influences that Jupiter has on Pisces take on a more subtle, inward role with Pisces, including the sign's creativity, imagination, and spirituality. Both Pisces and Sagittarius can get very similar benefits from Jupiter, but they will manifest differently between the contemplative, reflective Pisces, and the outgoing, bold Sagittarius. Venus is exalted in Pisces because she combines well with the sign's sensitive and spiritual nature. Therefore, those born under Venus in Pisces can have the best of both these highly agreeable planetary energies.

## Personality Traits

Folks born under the sign of Pisces are introspective individuals who like to stay subtle while being very selfless. This inward-oriented sign is deeply contemplative and invested in matters of philosophy, spirituality, and soul-searching. Being the last of the twelve, Pisces also often possesses various traits that can be found in the previous eleven signs. Pisces is a rare breed because they manage to be selfless and sacrificial as they are so focused on their inner questions and journey.

Pisces folks also are very emotional, which doesn't necessarily translate as expressive. Simply put, Pisces are attuned to their own feelings and those of others, but it's something that they subtly contemplate on the inside, like most other things. Pisces are often the person who feels other people's pain but also loves to share in their happiness and joy. Pisces is also a sign that relies heavily on intuition, which is usually highly developed for those born under this sign.

And so, the greatest strengths that Pisces has included their contemplation, empathy, and spiritual maturity. What's more, Pisces excels at sharing these strengths with the world and providing guidance to others. Coupled with creativity, this nature is what makes them good artists, especially poets, painters, and musicians. Pisces make natural advisors and counselors, and one of their greatest satisfactions is to heal another person, especially emotionally and spiritually.

As you can imagine, Pisces' tenderness, compassion, and emotional nature can also be weaknesses if they are unchecked. Pisces can sometimes be too sensitive and take things to heart even when they shouldn't. In the case of artistic Pisces, their preoccupation with their abstract ideas and dreams can make them lose sight of reality, leading to financial and other struggles. However, a Pisces who pursues an artist's lifestyle will often not care about their material wellbeing. A path of spiritual and emotional fulfillment with complete disregard for material gain is one that some Pisces will consciously choose. There, it's a matter of personal priority and not necessarily a weakness. Problems will arise if other people must rely on them. One of the greatest pitfalls that Pisces must watch out for is escapism.

## Compatibility

Water and earth signs are the ones that Pisces finds most agreeable. Pisces' compatibility with other water signs is reflected in the level of emotional understanding and deeper communication that is possible in these relationships. As with most other signs, Pisces can function very well with other people born under the same sign, but it's their very similarity that might eventually lead to problems. Pisces will relate incredibly well with most Cancers because they share a lot in the way of interests, feelings, and overall lifestyle. The relationship between these two will be one that's full of care, commitment, and understanding, so the bond will run deep.

Scorpio complements Pisces quite well, too, particularly by encouraging them to show more initiative and leave their comfort zone.

Pisces' emotional nature and a knack for philosophical concepts will benefit from relationships with earth signs because these folks will have a way of keeping Pisces grounded just enough to balance things out. With Pisces, the practical Capricorn will learn how to embrace their own inner mysteries, sparking their introspective interest. In return, Capricorn can help Pisces articulate and materialize many of their philosophical concepts that might otherwise be difficult to understand. Pisces is in polarity with Virgo, which can lead to a strong opposite attraction or conflict. Usually though, the two will make a good couple or a team. Taurus is another great match for a strong relationship, especially regarding passion and pleasure, which both signs seek.

Pisces will have trouble getting along with most people who fall under fire signs. Quite simply, Pisces likes privacy and will often need to retreat and enjoy some peace and quiet. Being impulsive and often volatile, fire signs can cause a lot of stress and friction in the world of Pisces. The assertive Aries, adventurous Sagittarius, and spotlight-loving Leo will often be more trouble than they are worth as far as Pisces is concerned. The disruption will be less extreme with air signs. Pisces might find these folks refreshing and highly stimulating, but it's likely that even air signs will be too changeable and hectic for Pisces' liking. In time, the thing that initially draws Pisces to one of the air signs can easily become the very thing that causes them to part ways.

## Love

One of Pisces' greatest gifts is that they can build a successful relationship with almost anyone if they are motivated to try hard enough. As we discussed above, they're not compatible with everyone, but they are perhaps more adept at surmounting differences than other signs are. Pisces fall in love easily and intensely when they meet the right person.

From the moment they enter a relationship or even as early as they have feelings for the person, Pisces will commit themselves fully. This is because Pisces generally have a no-nonsense attitude with relationships. They don't want to waste any time with meaningless flings or games and will rather get to work immediately, building something that's valuable and durable.

Pisces are very emotional and romantic, but their real emotional depth is demonstrated in their knack for understanding others' emotions, especially those closest to them. Pisces is, perhaps, without competition when it comes to how much they would sacrifice for the one they love. There is virtually no length they wouldn't go to to protect, support, and cherish their partner. It's rare for Pisces to do or say anything to make it clear to their partner that they want the same level of devotion, but that doesn't mean they don't want it.

## Other Relationships

Based on this, it shouldn't be difficult for you to imagine what Pisces is like with their cherished friends and family. While they might not be as focused on building a home as Cancers, Pisces undoubtedly have an extraordinary level of devotion to their family. This goes beyond just the immediate family they might be living with. Pisces enjoys spending time with relatives and another extended family, so they look forward to gatherings.

Because of their devotion, loyalty, and especially because of their heightened empathy, Pisces are very valuable as friends. Even when they have their own problems, Pisces is the person who goes around solving all their friends' problems, giving them the best advice, and always being available to at least hear out their woes. Folks with a close Pisces friend might as well save the money they would have used on a therapist, unless their problems are more than just the blues. This caring, giving nature is why Pisces forget all about themselves and their own problems.

Worse yet, there are those who seek to exploit Pisces because of their kindness. Therefore, it's important for the fish to practice assertiveness. This is something they should especially be careful about in the workplace or on various business endeavors. Unless they learn how to assert their wishes occasionally and fight for what they deserve, Pisces can easily be passed over and miss out on many opportunities at work.

## Work

Creativity and people skills are perhaps the main Pisces strengths valued most highly in the workplace. Depending on the job at hand, these qualities can go a long way. However, what's almost guaranteed is that Pisces will be well-liked at their job because they're helpful and easy to get along with. In general, Pisces will benefit from a work arrangement that allows them to have some freedom to improvise and get creative. Pisces will do well on jobs that depend on creativity and imagination. But the fish will enjoy helping, healing, and otherwise supporting others. While Pisces don't enjoy stringent routine, they don't bode well in risky, fast-paced, or otherwise stressful jobs either.

Pisces must put in some effort to find the perfect job for them. Some Pisceans will get lucky in that regard, while others must do their best to adapt and compromise, at least to some extent. The third option, which Pisces sometimes choose, is to essentially create their own job. If they can adapt to a hectic schedule, Pisces have done well as nurses, physicians, or other healthcare personnel. It's the care for other people that attract Pisces to healthcare and makes them adapt. Pisceans often engage in various forms of private or one-on-one therapy.

## Getting Along with a Pisces

As you can see, getting along with a Pisces isn't difficult. Even as a completely new face, you can have meaningful, personal conversations with Pisces. They will give you the time of day and hear you out as if you've known each other for years, and they will give you the best advice they can. On top of that, they are more than willing to help strangers with concrete action, too, if it's needed. Pisces' willingness to freely express what they're truly feeling and thinking, whether it's positive or negative, also contributes to the ease of interaction with this sign.

There are two potential problems in the interaction between Pisces and other people. The first one, which we've already discussed in length, is that they can give away more than they're taking. This also is one of the few things they won't openly talk about. In the interest of fairness and kindness, it's your duty to make sure that you aren't taking advantage of Pisces, whether they're a friend, coworker, or romantic partner. The second issue is their dreamy nature, because of which they sometimes focus more on abstract ideas and dreams than actions. This can be an issue in the workplace, but it's nothing that can't be solved through conversation.

# Conclusion

Once you get a good grip on each of the signs' basics, you will have a new set of tools to help you chart your path through life a little bit better. Both the situations and the people you run into will make a lot more sense when you know a thing or two about the subtle, invisible forces that influence us all behind the scenes.

Besides all the information about each of the twelve signs and how they impact people's personalities, something else that you should take away from this book is that astrology doesn't imply hard determinism. The astrological influences we have discussed are mostly just that - influences. They can set a newly born soul on a certain path, but the choices this person makes and the effort they put in later, can still determine the outcome.

The information you've gathered in this book should help you get a better understanding of what's behind some virtues and flaws you see in yourself and others. The same applies to many of those irrational aspects of our lives, actions, and responses to experiences, whether they are negative or positive.

Astrological interpretations are not intended to discourage you or make you give up on trying to change yourself and your life for the better. Quite on the contrary, this ancient wisdom helps you on your way toward accomplishing your goals, becoming the best version of yourself, and enriching your life with people with whom you are compatible. I hope it will also help you understand the relationships you can't choose - between you and your family members - at least a little bit better. Some things, especially people, are beyond our control, though, and astrology will help you come to terms with that in a healthy, constructive way.

# Part 2: Moon Signs

*The Ultimate Guide to Understanding Your Sign, Different Sun-Moon Astrology Combinations, and Compatibility*

# Introduction

Have you ever read your sign's horoscope and thought the description did not sound like you? Or perhaps the information was completely irrelevant to where you were in life? Did you know that you must look beyond the Sun sign? If you would like to have a bigger picture, you must focus on your Moon sign.

Or perhaps someone asked you what your Zodiac sign was, and you immediately replied with yours. To your surprise, your friend didn't believe you were a Sagittarius. To her, you were a Pisces or Libra.

Usually, someone is referring to your Sun sign when a person asks you, "What sign are you?" And while this is perfectly acceptable to ask because the Sun sign does offer others a glimpse of your personality and what traits you show to the world, there is more than an individual can ask to get a clearer picture of who you are.

Your friend's words probably resonated with you, and you decided it was time to get your research gloves on. You soon realized something called a Moon sign, and the more you investigate it, the more you feel like you are not a Sagittarius.

You probably didn't feel like the horoscope was talking to you in the first place, because even though your birthdate says you are a Sagittarius—or that your Sun sign is in Sagittarius—you felt more like a Pisces person. You are very emotional, and you have a deep connection with going under the water and discovering your true inner world.

This happens because you have a Pisces Moon. For the horoscope to depict an accurate image of you, you must know your Moon sign, which is not always referenced.

However, you may wonder why the Moon sign is important. Well, did you know that the Moon has different phases and that all of them will, undoubtedly, alter your perception by making you more in tune with nature? Were you aware that the Moon's phases even make the ocean's tides increase or decrease?

The important thing to notice is that both the Sun and Moon signs need one another to maintain a healthy lifestyle. You cannot have one without the other. They work together to form your whole self.

Even though at first glimpse, the Moon seems like it is constantly transforming itself and moving from one side to another, whereas the Sun is simply there just being the Sun, this is not entirely true.

It is not like the Moon constantly changes throughout the month; it's more of a case of perception: your perception of the Moon changes continuously during the month. Hence, sometimes you see a big Full Moon, and other times, you don't see it at all, or you only see half of it. It's not that the Moon is not there; it's more to do with the darkened areas that are not illuminated for you to see them.

There are eight Moon phases:

- The New Moon is when the Moon is not visible at all.
- A Waxing Crescent Moon is when there is a very thin crescent on the Moon's left side.

- First-quarter is when the first quarter of the Moon can be seen—also referred to as the Half-moon.

- Waxing Gibbous is the growing phase between the Half-moon or First-quarter and the Full Moon. Waxing is synonymous with increasing sizes or getting bigger.

- Full Moon is when you can see the whole Moon.

- Waning Gibbous is the phase between the Full Moon and Half-moon again. Waning is synonymous with decreasing sizes or getting smaller.

- The third quarter is when the Moon is half again. It shows in contrary to the First quarter of the Moon.

- Waning Crescent is when there is a very thin crescent phase on the Moon's right side.

It takes almost twenty-eight days for the Moon to orbit around Earth. When this happens, the Moon will complete its cycle. If you divide 28 by twelve—as in twelve different Sun signs—you will get two point three: the number of days the Moon will spend on each Moon sign. As a result, the Moon will also give you a sign, which is your Moon sign.

But first, you will start at the beginning, so you are crystal clear about things.

What is a Sun sign? The Sun sign is usually synonymous with the Zodiac sign, as most people interpret it that way. The Sun sign will tell you what the Sun's position was at the moment you were born. As a result, there are twelve Sun signs because there are twelve months in a year. A person can only be one Sun sign and one Moon sign, but that does not mean that you cannot have characteristics from other signs in your birth—or natal—chart.

Also, a different planet is actively ruling each Sun sign, and this will also have direct consequences on your personality traits or choices. For example, Gemini is ruled by Mercury, which is known for bringing intellectual characteristics to those born under that Sun sign.

Think of a natal chart as if you were taking a picture of the sky and the universe, exactly at the moment you were born. All those planets and signs will depict your personality and your life.

So, what is a Moon sign? The Moon sign tells you the position of the Moon at the time you were born. The main differences between Sun and Moon signs are that Sun signs will display your personality traits and how your character is, whereas Moon signs will display how you are doing with your emotional side, what moods you have, how you manage your instincts, and what subconscious behaviors you believe in.

In other words, the Sun sign is the outer shell, and the Moon sign is the inner shell.

For example, Taurus is passionate, outgoing, and loves pleasure and things related to the earth. If a Taurus has a Pisces Moon, they will become introspective, they will enjoy the desires expressed in their dreams, and they will focus more on the inner depths of their personality.

However, if a Taurus has a different Moon sign, they will display a distinct set of characteristics from a Taurus Pisces. This will make them more unique than ever.

Another basic difference between Sun and Moon signs is this: If you would like to know your Sun sign, you only need to know your birth date. If you would like to know your Moon sign, you need to know your birth date, the time, and the place you were born.

This can be explained simply: The Sun usually takes longer, more precisely, thirty days to transition from one-star sign—or Sun sign—onto the next, but the Moon moves faster than the Sun, and it will only stay in one particular sign for two and a half days at a time. So, it is more challenging to discover the Moon sign because there is a need for more detailed information to get an accurate reading.

How can a person calculate their Moon sign? You can find your Moon sign by using an online program or a special table that will allow you to see where the Moon was transitioning through the moment you were born.

When doing so, you will first need to write when you were born. Write down the date, month, and year. You can use many online calculators, and you can also contact an astrologer to help you.

You need all this information because the Moon's position depends entirely on where you were born. If you were born in Asia, your Moon would be in one position, and if you were born in South America, your Moon would be on the other side. If you do not have this information, you can always put the nearest place or time you think would be good. It will not give you an accurate description, but it could help regardless.

The results you get are your natal chart. There, you will discover your Moon sign, but you will soon realize there are many "houses." These are the ones that represent different areas or stages of life. They also offer you a glimpse of how you respond to those situations and express your emotions.

For example, a person with a Sagittarius Moon in the ninth house will likely feel great when they successfully explore something new and become a master. This is because the ninth house represents expansion, and the planet Jupiter, which is known for all things great, also governs Sagittarius.

This is an important aspect within the astrology world because you are an individual who likes to differentiate yourself from the rest of the crowd. But you first need to discover your Sun and Moon signs to do the rest of your birth chart.

Getting to know oneself is a never-ending process in which parts of your past are constantly appearing and waving at you. However, it also offers you the opportunity to see how you can shape your future, starting right now. When you are aware of your Moon sign, you notice a different side of you, and you will broaden your perspective towards life and consciously form your path.

It is fair to say that all human beings have different ways of experiencing life. Everyone is built with a wide range of characteristics that shape their entire existence. They have different strengths and weaknesses, and almost everyone is actively trying to understand why they behave the way they do.

Each Zodiac Sun sign has its characteristics, so it is not surprising to find these sets of traits on the Moon signs. For example, an Aries Moon means that the person is very passionate, and they have plenty of energy to go through life's most difficult situations. Or if you have a Virgo Moon, the chances are you are very witty and intelligent, and you prefer to pay attention to the smallest of details instead of looking at the biggest picture.

Once you recognize who you truly are, what you want in life, and what you need to improve, you will also realize who you are and how you are becoming yourself–and knowing your Moon sign can help you achieve all of this.

So, what are the Moon signs? Why are they important in modern astrology? What do they tell people about their personalities and ways of looking at life? Here you will learn about the different and possible 144 combinations between Sun and Moon signs.

This information is relevant for any inner journey, as you will soon discover whether your Sun and Moon signs are at peace or if there is friction between them. Sun and Moon signs can complement one another or not work together at all. That is why individuals will have more problems trying to overcome life situations because their Sun and Moon signs are not balanced.

As a result, perhaps some Sun and Moon sign combinations are excellent, whereas others will probably face more challenging situations.

As its title indicates, this book is an ultimate guide to understanding your sign, different Sun-Moon astrology combinations, and compatibility. If you would truly like to find out what your personality is like, and most importantly, why it is the way it is, you need to know your Sun and Moon signs.

Once you gather this information, you can work toward improving yourself. You can amend the differences between both signs, and you can join them in strength. It is important to be aware of all the different parts of your chart, not just the Sun and Moon sign.

If you have already discovered the world behind the Sun signs, it is time to jump into the Moon sign. This book will guide you through this alternative universe filled with information.

Are you ready? Time to travel to the Moon.

# Chapter 1: Aries Moon

**Symbol**: The Ram

**Element**: Fire

**Quality**: Cardinal

**Ruling House:** First

**Ruling Planet**: Mars

## A Brief Explanation of the Moon in Aries

Aries is the first sign of the Zodiac. As a result, it leads the way for the rest of the signs to follow. If you are an Aries Moon, you are likely a fiery and impulsive individual who truly knows what you want and how to get it.

Aries is a cardinal sign, and this means you love to set things in motion. You are a natural-born leader, and one of your biggest qualities is to be the first to do many things in life.

As an Aries Moon, you will often feel you need something else, even if you do not need it at all. It is more of a case of fulfilling something or achieving something. An Aries Moon will often make you feel emotionally satisfied whenever you are going through an exciting time or change.

An Aries Moon is the one that gives impulse to the rest of the signs. However, you are also likely rushing into doing things because you do not stop to think, *What am I about to do*? You just do it.

The planet Mars rules Aries, which, in turn, is the planet behind wards and aggressive behavior. As a result, many Aries feel like they are temperamental for no reason or that they like to fight unnecessary battles all the time.

Lastly, Aries will always say "Yes" to adventures, ideas, and activities. Your Moon will make you explore unknown areas of life, and you will make everyone else follow along with your fiery and incredibly charming personality.

## Aries Moon and Your Personality Traits

## Aries Moon Strengths

### You are a Natural-born and Active Leader

As an Aries Moon, you will never tell others to do something without having done it yourself first. So, you are an outstanding leader because you are also aware of the influence you have on others.

Another important aspect of being an active leader is that you easily overcome obstacles, whereas others may think it's impossible to go through them. If you have a difficult situation and you do not know what to do, Aries can work it out for you.

### You are Self-Confident

Your Aries Moon will make you always believe in yourself, and you are proud of what you are doing. Having this Moon makes you know your worth, and your self-esteem is healthy.

### You Irradiate Positive Energy

Even through the darkest of times, an Aries Moon will always smile. Thus, you will think it is necessary to go through troubling situations because this is the only way you can learn to come through a storm.

An Aries Moon is a very active sign. Hence, you are also spreading positive energy toward everything you do.

### You are a Creative Human Being

An Aries Moon will always find something exciting to do, even if they have done the same thing a million times already. You are so unique that you come up with great ideas that other people will sometimes not understand.

## Aries Moon Weaknesses

### You Get Angry Easily

But can you blame yourself? You are the first sign of the Zodiac, but you are also a fire and cardinal sign. Of course, you will get angry as soon as the opportunity comes your way. However, different Moon Signs will help an Aries Moon overcome this issue—or at least work on it.

### You are Very Impatient

An Aries Moon person wants everything done by yesterday. You will not rest until you accomplish your goals, and you will become more impatient than ever if obstacles get in your way. Aries Moon wants everything as quickly and won't mind pushing others away to achieve everything they have imagined.

### You are Very Selfish

An Aries Moon is not known for selfless acts—quite the opposite occurs. Usually, if an Aries Moon is behind something, it is because they can get something out of it.

### You Love Attention

Aries are attention seekers too, which makes you feel frustrated when no one pays attention to you, and what you are doing or saying. It almost seems like your Moon in Aries needs to be the center of attention, or you won't perform at all.

## Aries Moon and Your Love Compatibility

The Aries Moon is a courageous leader who loves freedom and love. Regardless of its Sun or Moon location, this fire sign usually has love compatibility with other Fire Moon signs (Leo and Sagittarius) or Air Moon signs (Gemini, Libra, and Aquarius).

As an Aries Moon, you probably recognized these traits. You need someone who can easily catch up with you, someone that encourages you to become a leader and who will always have your back. However, you also need someone who is not afraid to tell you when you are making a mistake, even if this action may bring future arguments between the two of you.

An Aries Moon will make you have strong fights with your loved ones; still, you will defend your arguments no matter what. As soon as those situations have faded away, you will have plenty of time to kiss and make up.

An Aries Moon is the one that dives first into new love relationships. It's like they are telling you not to be afraid of jumping toward exciting encounters. You know that a friend can also become something more.

Your Aries Moon is less compatible with a Cancer Moon. A Cancer Moon will think of an Aries Moon as detached from a real person, someone who does not want to work alongside them to achieve a healthier relationship—and perhaps you won't. But you do not want them telling you so. On the opposite hand, an Aries Moon will think of Cancer as too clingy and they need space from them—not a good combo.

# Aries as a Sun Sign and the Different Moon Signs

### Aries Sun + Aries Moon

If there is one sign that truly symbolizes fire, Aries is the one. So, can you imagine what a double Aries is like since you are one? Fire everywhere. Double Aries makes you a feisty person, so you will say everything as it is—or at least how you see it—and you will not be afraid to speak your mind, sometimes even louder than the rest.

As a double Aries, you have emotional intensity like no other sign. Sometimes, you are not even aware of this powerful combination and how it can come across to others. Hence, you can hurt another person's feelings without knowing it.

### Aries Sun + Taurus Moon

A Taurus Moon brings a sense of grounding to the Aries Sun sign. Your Taurus Moon makes you more patient, so you are perfectly fine when you must wait, as you consider it as part of life.

It almost seems like the Taurus Moon urges you to slow down and look around to embrace nature and its changes. Also, because Taurus comes right after Aries, perhaps the Bull already knows what to expect from you—fire, and more fire.

### Aries Sun + Gemini Moon

An Aries Sun and Gemini Moon mean that you like to chat. When these two signs are combined, you become someone expressive, and you are not afraid to speak your mind.

Also, Gemini is an air sign, so the fleeing air can calm your Aries fire's intensity. Hence, you have a more relaxed and heartfelt communication style. But the other way around can happen, and your Aries will have a stronger fire in no time—which usually translates to you being straightforward and unafraid of speaking the truth.

### Aries Sun + Cancer Moon

When Cancer Moon appears in Aries, you can be deeply sensitive. Hence why you follow your emotions too closely and sometimes avoid looking at the bigger picture.

Besides this, the combination highly depends on your daily emotions. If a feeling is too strong or you don't have the right tools to understand it, it can also bring much frustration and resentment.

### Aries Sun + Leo Moon

This combination is a hot temper alert. It would be best if you exercise as a way of releasing heat and energies. You are proud of your level of intensity and what you can achieve with it.

However, you are also a person who likes things your way, with little to no room to compromise. You will only look at yourself, and you can get caught up in your flames. This could be a troublesome situation for some, but you seem to find your path every time.

### Aries Sun + Virgo Moon

You love helping others. Sometimes you even forget about yourself, much to the amazement of other Aries combinations. Virgos forget about their emotions regularly. Thus, there could be a constant struggle between your Aries Sun and the Virgo Moon.

Aries will need to remind you it is okay to make mistakes, as Virgo can become a hypercritical sign with yourself or others.

### Aries Sun + Libra Moon

These two signs are the first opposite signs on the Zodiac wheel. You are almost always trying to balance how you feel, your desires, and what you would like to share with others. Within this combination, either the Sun or Moon sign will make the other feel safe.

A Libra Moon is usually someone who looks after others and something your Aries Sun is not very familiar with. Not only do they want to help others, but they also do so expecting nothing in return. This intentional yet free giving is something new to you.

### Aries Sun + Scorpio Moon

Talk about a powerful and sexy combination of signs. These two signs are highly sexual beings, and it should not be surprising since you love experiencing new things in the bedroom.

You know when to rely on your intuition on every single level. Still, you will also feel the need to innovate, so this combination brings the better of two worlds—what is on the inside and how you can move forward and become a leader.

### Aries Sun + Sagittarius Moon

If there were a sign combination that likes to travel far, this would be it. That is why you are probably flying around in their double fire. These two signs make you as eclectic as you can be, and you're not afraid to show it.

You're always aiming for more. It is not enough to just travel. You need to learn the language, live with the locals, and discover many other hidden gems that the rest of the world is unaware of. The further you can go, the more invested you are.

### Aries Sun + Capricorn Moon

This combination could present setbacks, mainly because there is always a struggle between Aries not being consistent and Capricorn trying to be steady with everything they do. As a result, your Capricorn Moon can take the lead over your Aries Sun, and you become a workaholic or very dependent on something.

Capricorn will shoot Aries's intensity to the roof, and you have nonstop desires to succeed and make a name for yourself. Lastly, it is important to express your emotions without feeling guilty.

### Aries Sun + Aquarius Moon

This combination is intense, and they like to get things done. Aries has a passion that Aquarius loves. Also, Aquarius needs to help others on a humanitarian level, and Aries has never encountered that before.

As a person born with these two signs, you are likely a straightforward person whose flames go toward solving the biggest problems they will forever encounter. You are highly independent, and it is sometimes difficult for you to allow others in and enjoy their company.

### Aries Sun + Pisces Moon

If you have this powerful combination, chances are you are a very spiritual person who is always trying to light the inner fire everyone has. This Aries is likely going to be more vulnerable than others, mainly because of your Pisces Moon, which makes you pour your soul out.

An Aries person with a Pisces Moon makes you someone who enjoys following your instincts and who would not look around to see what the others are doing. You will only swim forward to your goals.

# Chapter 2: Taurus Moon

**Symbol:** The Bull

**Element:** Earth

**Quality:** Fixed

**Ruling House:** Second

**Ruling Planet:** Venus

## A Brief Explanation of the Moon in Taurus

The Bull is known for being an energetic animal in a constant struggle between being relaxed or ready to go.

A Taurus Moon makes you struggle with these feelings because, on the one hand, you are very independent and confident about what you are doing. On the other hand, you're usually very stubborn, and asking for help is not something you're used to doing.

If Aries Moon is a leader, Taurus Moon makes you the one that plans and invites others to participate in what is coming. If you have a Taurus Moon, you are likely always searching for your truth.

Sometimes you can be so determined about doing something that you won't mind moving people, places, or situations away from yourself if that means you will accomplish what you set your mind to.

Also, Taurus belongs to the fixed signs' quality. This can sum up what you want for your life: a home, security, and stability. If you do something, it is because you feel like doing it. If you help someone, it's because you genuinely want to do so.

Taurus Moon is very sensual, and it is perfectly normal for you to be diving in a sea of sexual explorations throughout your life. It's also common to see your Taurus Moon being everybody else's rock. You are very loyal to who you are and who you want to become.

## Taurus Moon and Your Personality Traits

### Taurus Moon Strengths

#### You are Organized

If you ever need to get something done quickly, call a Taurus Moon. They will probably know what and how to do it in no time.

So, you are very organized. You know when you need to build your dreams because only you are responsible for your success in life.

#### You are Consistent

If a Taurus person falls nine times, they will likely get up ten times, if not more.

This Moon makes you a know-it-all—but only because you enjoy your learning journey since you want to become someone others admire. If you ever feel lost, it is thanks to your Taurus Moon; however, you will quickly go back to your path. No matter how many times this may occur, you are truthful to yourself.

### You are Straightforward

Taurus Moon is not afraid to speak his or her mind. You encourage others to do so too. A Taurus Moon makes you have a powerful impact on others, and you usually take advantage of this by influencing others positively.

### You are Patient

A Taurus Moon knows when it is the right time to act. You seek the right opportunities, and you seize the moment. This characteristic, coupled with organizational skills, can make a Taurus Moon go far in life, especially when you won't rest until you are successful.

## Taurus Moon Weaknesses

### You are Temperamental

A Taurus Moon makes you have a strong temper. It is normal for you to flare and cause trouble, even if you are not right. A Taurus Moon does not mind getting into a fight, especially if they are defending their views or someone else who is less advantaged in life.

### You are Stubborn

This is something relatively normal in a Taurus, but your Taurus Moon brings more stubbornness to the picture. On top of it, a Taurus Moon is a fixed sign, so it feels like you are always trying to prove your point. But regardless of what others may think about it, you will stomp your foot.

### You Often Detach Yourself from the Rest

Taurus Moon can be too detached sometimes. So, you will put yourself first, and then there is the rest of the world. You may seem emotionally detached or even uninterested in what is surrounding you.

### You Don't Like Change

More often than you would like to admit, your Taurus Moons will make you feel as if changes are too difficult to go through. You may think you are protecting yourself from problems, so you prefer to avoid recent changes. If others impose a change and you don't agree with it, all hell could break loose in a matter of seconds.

## Taurus Moon and Your Love Compatibility

The Taurus Moon is someone who values security, knows what they want, and thinks life should always be enjoyable. Regardless of its Sun or Moon location, this earth sign usually has love compatibility with other earth Moon signs (Virgo and Capricorn) or water Moon signs (Pisces, Cancer, Scorpio).

A Taurus Moon needs someone who can make life sexy, has a strong inner drive to become a better person, and is not afraid to listen to them and join their cause.

Your Taurus Moon is likely going to the end of the world if it means that you will protect and defend your way of thinking. You are so stubborn that you won't even mind losing friendships along the way if you stay committed to the truth.

A Taurus Moon is the one that seeks sensuality and sexual chemistry with others. When you start a new love relationship, you are especially not afraid of embracing your sexuality, as it means you will have a great time exploring with another person.

A Taurus Moon is less compatible with a Sagittarius Moon. The fire sign will probably want to travel the world or explore new cultures. In contrast, Taurus would like to explore their safety zone, whether Sagittarius likes it or not. Sagittarius may also feel like they have compromised themselves by being in a relationship with Taurus, but the Bull will probably think Sagittarius is never doing enough to make the relationship thrive.

# Taurus as a Sun Sign and the Different Moon Signs

### Taurus Sun + Aries Moon

There is an interesting chemistry between these two signs. Even though Taurus follows Aries, the latter is impatient that Taurus feels the need to move away faster than ever.

Having an Aries Moon means that Taurus is more in touch with your fire, and your emotions could come to the surface. This is a noble thing, especially if Taurus hides away your feelings or if you become too emotionally secluded.

### Taurus Sun + Taurus Moon

A double Taurus is one of the most stubborn people on Earth. Yet, these signs make you one of the most strong-minded and reliable individuals you will ever meet. You are very confident in yourself, and you will consistently try to improve your life.

Being double Taurus is like having double fun, double compromise, and double stubbornness. You will not rest at all until you materialize your dreams. You will need to be careful when spending too much time by yourself, though, as you hide from the rest of the world from time to time.

### Taurus Sun + Gemini Moon

There is a unique balance in this combination. On the one hand, your Taurus Sun is known for working extra hard all the time. Your Gemini loves to communicate everything they can, so they will always move toward achieving their life goals together.

This duo's energy is incredible, mainly because your Gemini Moon helps Taurus feel more at ease with the decisions you have to make. Though, the Bull will help Gemini feel more confident by giving them a much-needed impulse.

**Taurus Sun + Cancer Moon**

This mix has a strong potential to make you a great friend and an intimate lover. Cancer is the one who loves nurturing and making others feel welcomed; Taurus is the one who enjoys getting all the attention—and you are perfectly aware of this.

Moreover, the water sign can make your Taurus feel even more adventurous regarding jumping into unknown territories—albeit with having the certainty that you will eventually get back home, where you belong.

**Taurus Sun + Leo Moon**

These two signs are fixed energies, and this can be extrapolated by your personality. Sometimes you crave the attention; other times, it's given to you. While Leo is a dramatic sign and makes you want to be the center of the world, there is always a chance of a war between these two ways of thinking.

You are loyal to those around you, and even though you may seem like you are tough on the outside, you are soft on the inside. You know your strengths well, and your weaknesses humble you.

**Taurus Sun + Virgo Moon**

You are a very curious person who has an inquisitive mind. By nature, you are the perfect definition of what an earth sign is: grounded. You love to serve others, and you work toward goals actively.

Virgos will make your Taurus feel safe concerning feelings, so you will try to express how you truly see life and how much you care for your loved ones.

**Taurus Sun + Libra Moon**

Venus rules both signs, so you are someone who has amazing and vibrant love energy. You are everybody's best friend; you love to get in touch with others and are very social.

The cool part about the combination between Taurus Sun and a Libra Moon is that all your characteristics align with your signs' interests. You are the quintessential artist, chef, or even mom or dad. Everything you do, you do with massive amounts of love.

**Taurus Sun + Scorpio Moon**

Having a Scorpio Moon is likely making you feel everything extra hard; your intensity levels are likely way up sometimes. This is because Taurus is very stubborn and constant; Scorpio is the passionate one who can also be stubborn and constant.

As a water sign, Scorpio will make your Taurus get out of their comfort zone, as this is the only way you can grow. Also, Taurus will bring a sense of emotional stability to Scorpio, so they become a powerful combination.

**Taurus Sun + Sagittarius Moon**

This combination asks the most important questions upfront without hesitating their intentions. You are known for being adventurous, down-to-earth, and a terrific storyteller. Sagittarius Moon will impulse your Taurus Sun to get out of their comfort zone. In contrast, Taurus will bring more grounded energy to Sagittarius's life.

One sign will try to impose their ways of seeing life onto the other sign. As a result, there is a real possibility of having a persistent inner struggle because they will both fight hard for your attention, no matter what.

**Taurus Sun + Capricorn Moon**

If these two signs are mixed, chances are you are not only the boss but very bossy. Taurus is always working hard to have a healthy bank account, and your Capricorn Moon is always investing time and effort into improving themselves.

You are completely focused on your career and social status. You may have problems trying to navigate your emotions, so it is advisable to explore your feelings.

### Taurus Sun + Aquarius Moon

When these two signs are combined, they will work hard to see justice in the world—or at least within themselves. Aquarius brings humanitarian energy that your Taurus has never experienced, and the Bull will give the air sign an important push as well.

Aquarius understands the importance of working together, something Taurus is still learning. You know you need to work on yourself first to help others at a later stage.

### Taurus Sun + Pisces Moon

A Pisces Moon always means that the person is very empathetic toward other people. This Moon will also make your Taurus Sun enjoy talking with others, and is a person who has understood the way they truly are and honors their life's path.

This combination is energetic, yet you are also flexible with everything that life throws at you. Pisces is a mutable sign, so this Moon will help your Taurus become less rigid—or fixed—and more in tune with your personal needs.

# Chapter 3: Gemini Moon

**Symbol:** The Twins

**Element:** Air

**Quality:** Mutable

**Ruling House:** Third

**Ruling Planet:** Mercury

## A Brief Explanation of the Moon in Gemini

When a Gemini Moon appears, they are usually the wittiest and funniest individuals ever. They are the ones who are not afraid to go into a room filled with strangers and make everyone remember who they are by the end of the night.

A Gemini Moon will make you own the place you are at, as it will make people love you. As a result, you form deep connections with others almost immediately.

This Moon sign makes you aware of your popularity, yet you also know that you are not going around asking for it. If you ask others how you became so popular, they probably won't even know what to tell you because they just loved you as you are.

You can adapt easily to any situation, group of people or challenges that may come your way. It seems like the Gemini Twins have two sets of eyes, brains, hands, and souls wherever they go. They can visualize everything; they are aware of what is happening around them, and they seem to be very down-to-earth.

A Gemini Moon also loves to talk. Mercury rules this sign, which, unsurprisingly, is the communications planet. When Mercury is in retrograde, you will feel it the most, regardless of whether the energy is positive or negative.

As a result, your Gemini Moon always knows when to communicate something—albeit sometimes you forget how to say things nicely. With Gemini, it is all black or white, day or night. You think too much, and you talk too much, and you do too much.

# Gemini Moon and Your Personality Traits

## Gemini Moon Strengths

### You Are Energetic

A Gemini Moon seems to have its energy at high levels all the time. Considering this is a mutable sign, you will change shapes to provide energetic results continually.

You know you need to work toward achieving your goals, and sometimes this feeling is so strong that you cannot stop performing or doing the things that will take you to the next level.

### You Adapt Easily to New Situations

Perhaps the combination between the Twins' sign and their planet ruler, Mercury, made you adaptable to different—sometimes even challenging—situations.

A true Gemini Moon adapts to people, situations, and places like no other sign. Sometimes your closest relationships will wonder if you are truly like this or putting on a show because you love to amaze people.

You know that change is inevitable, so you need to be ready for it.

### Your Imagination Runs Wild

Your mind never stops, and you are always doing something creative and artful. The more creative it gets, the better.

A Gemini Moon loves when others listen to you or when you amazingly see what you have created. It is expected for you to develop the greatest ideas or stories, create new trends, and express yourself in a million different ways.

### You are Emotionally Intelligent

A Gemini Moon knows how to read another person's mood without having to ask. You are aware of what others expect of you, but you do not care about that either.

You understand that your mood is forever changing, and you will display your true personality throughout the day. You are also empathetic and make sure everyone feels safe—at least when they are around you.

## Gemini Moon Weaknesses

### You Don't Know When to Stop

You cannot stop talking. You cannot stop feeling. You cannot stop being creative. This Moon is a nonstop sign, which can be exhausting to you and those around you. It almost feels like your mind is in a constant race with the rest of your body.

It is common for a Gemini Moon to make you feel like the entire weight is on your shoulders because you have created this situation for yourself. It's part of who you are.

### You Need to Communicate Everything

Often, you do not know how to remain silent. This could be a real issue, especially when working or in a relationship with a calmer and more serious Moon sign.

A Gemini Moon makes you think that everybody is ready to listen to you, and everyone wants to do so. You are often asked if you can quiet your mind.

### You Avoid Commitment

For you, love is a commitment. A Gemini Moon will be the first one to make you jump when someone asks you out on a date, but you will also be the first one to get out when your love relationship goes to interesting and more compromised places.

Commitment is not impossible under a Gemini Moon, but it takes work on your behalf to overcome these limiting beliefs. This is often a struggle for people born under this sign since you are not even aware that you react a certain way.

### You Hide Your True Colors

Perhaps it is because you are a mutable sign and because you're the Twins. When one of the twins is tired or not in the mood, the other can easily jump in. As a result, sometimes it may be difficult to understand who a Gemini Moon truly is.

It is normal for you to be an expert on something one day, and the following day, ask others the important questions because, according to you, you know nothing. You are always going back and forth, not only with yourself but also with your life.

## Gemini Moon and Your Love Compatibility

The Gemini Moon makes you someone who values creativity, crystal clear communications, and the ability to express emotions. Regardless of its Sun or Moon location, this sign usually has love compatibility with other Air Moon signs (Libra, Aquarius) or Fire Moon signs (Aries, Leo, Sagittarius).

A Gemini Moon makes you need someone who can communicate like you do, has a strong inner drive to explore new depths, and is not afraid to listen to you and ask the important questions.

A Gemini Moon means you are great at describing your feelings but not so great at feeling them; hence, you need someone to help you feel a great deal.

A Gemini Moon will inspire you to become the first to communicate your thoughts and then do the rest. You are not afraid of your crazy ideas. On the contrary, the weirder and wilder you are, the more you feel attracted to a person, like a true Gemini Moon. These feelings could be shared best with a Sagittarius Moon person.

Conversely, a Gemini Moon is less compatible with an Earth Moon sign. The earth sign will probably want to stay where they are, with all the comfort in the world. However, the Gemini Moon is always ready to conquer the next adventure.

In romance, your Gemini Moon and a Capricorn Moon could have their expiration day: your Moon will make you look the other way around when the Capricorn Moon constantly reminds you to be more serious.

## Gemini as a Sun Sign and the Different Moon Signs

### Gemini Sun + Aries Moon

This combination is a strong-minded individual who is confident and quick to respond. You know what you want, and you will scream at it for the world to hear exactly what it is. Fire takes over this time, and you are emotionally and communicatively fiery.

You are fixated in action—albeit that fixation can make you change your goals every other month because of your sign's quality of being mutable. The Twins see this in the fire counterpart and are completely thrilled about continuously pursuing that change of mind.

### Gemini Sun + Taurus Moon

You are very patient, and your Taurus Moon makes you likely to think twice before making your mind up. It differs completely from the Bull's precedent, Aries. The Moon in Taurus usually shows a steady-going grounding force and complements your Gemini very well.

These two signs will bring a balanced force to your life because the Moon in Taurus makes the Twins get their act together and do what needs to be done. The Twins also make the Bull communicate more healthily, as Taurus can be someone who shuts down from others.

**Gemini Sun + Gemini Moon**

This combination could present issues for you. You have two sets of Twins–four people, four souls, and four choices if you think about it. It can be challenging, as you will take everything to extreme levels.

A double air sign flies around their feelings and will communicate it in an intense yet calm manner. The catch here is that you avoid feeling. For you, it is easier to talk, draw, and materialize it than go through each of your emotions completely.

**Gemini Sun + Cancer Moon**

A true Gemini loves their independence. When the Twins are combined with a Cancer moon, they are suddenly interested in others, usually those closest to them. Cancer begins to empathize with others, something you had struggled to do so before, and your Gemini will learn that there is more room for emotions if only you allow it.

This combination brings something magical to the air, as you communicate well, and you actively work together to make life less serious and feel more peace.

**Gemini Sun + Leo Moon**

What happens when you combine signs that love the spotlight? They could either fight it or share it. Gemini and Leo decide to do the latter: they share everything. As a result, you are vocal about everything in life. You simply cannot do something quiet for only yourself to enjoy. You need to communicate it, and you do so in a vividly yet showy way.

Leo is very loyal to everyone, and your Gemini will have to learn about this relevant characteristic, especially when you have two choices to consider.

### Gemini Sun + Virgo Moon

If Gemini is the Twins, Virgo is the Mother who is always cleaning after her children. Virgo has a meticulous personality, making you feel this way, which is something new to you.

You will make others prove themselves before you feel relaxed and confident enough to let them know they are worthy of your ideas. Besides, you usually keep to yourself how you truly feel, as you value secrecy.

### Gemini Sun + Libra Moon

Both are air signs that love and feel at ease when communicating how they feel. As a result, your Gemini feels more relaxed and confident now that Libra is listening to the Twins' ideas. On an emotional level, Libra loves the exclusivity Gemini provides them with.

This combination makes you want to chat. You are that friend who is always talking but has very interesting things to say. However, you also know that silence is priceless, and you are conscious of the power behind your concise phrases.

### Gemini Sun + Scorpio Moon

This combination is all about following your intuition. Sometimes you will compete with yourself whenever you try to read another person. "Will my observations be on point?" is a question you often ask yourself.

You know how to set boundaries, especially when your freedom is being compromised. You are not afraid to speak your mind, but you will kindly ask others to swim the other way around if you do not see their point of view.

**Gemini Sun + Sagittarius Moon**

If your friends feel like going on a trip, they will call you. The fire that comes out of Sagittarius is more like a noble flame that is constantly going. It will feed the Twins' inquisitive nature with their adventurous side.

You want to talk with others, and you want others to talk with you. You are very open-minded and enjoy being with others. Your optimistic levels are sometimes over the roof, but you will try the best you can to achieve your dreams—and often, you are very lucky.

**Gemini Sun + Capricorn Moon**

Capricorn Moons love consistency and emotional stability, something Gemini is known to lack. You could benefit from their different energies, yet they will always have a constant inner battle. It is like you are stuck and do not know where to go most of the time.

Still, this earth sign will allow your Twins to feel more connected with the world; hence, why you come up with really controversial ideas because you are learning to reconcile your wild, adventurous side with your down-to-earth way of looking at life.

**Gemini Sun + Aquarius Moon**

This is another double air sign pair. A person born with this combination fights for their ideals. They do not sit down and watch the rest of the world take it on; they want to start a revolution.

Yet, an Aquarius moon will give you a more holistic view of life, where fellow individuals join to make the world a better place. Overall, you are very passionate and not afraid to show your emotions.

### Gemini Sun + Pisces Moon

You are an artist because you have such a creative combination. A Pisces Moon will allow your Gemini to swim through their ideas and take them to shore to become realities.

Gemini will also allow Pisces to show them the way, something unique for the Twins as they are used to taking the lead most of the time. A person with these signs always finds an impactful way of sharing how they feel.

# Chapter 4: Cancer Moon

**Symbol**: The Crab

**Element**: Water

**Quality**: Cardinal

**Ruling House**: Fourth

**Ruling Planet**: Moon

## A Brief Explanation of the Moon in Cancer

A Moon in Cancer means you are very sensitive, and you follow your intuition from an early age. As a cardinal sign, you know you are the beginning of something. You are the one that starts the changes so others can soon follow.

However, you are often portrayed as a distant individual, mainly because you prefer to keep your privacy to yourself–and it is often misunderstood.

A Cancer Moon will make you feel deeply worried about your loved ones, and you will tend to close yourself down before a new person tries to join in your life.

As a Cancer Moon, you know how to flow even among the most difficult situations life has put in your way. The Moon rules you, which also governs the water element.

You are always guided by what feels right, and you follow your intuition no matter what, even if others are telling you to run the other way.

But this could also mean that you have become intolerant to how others perceive life, and you will not even let them know this. You will drift away, your way. You do this because you prefer to avoid conflict; you think it is unnecessary, especially when you focus on other, more important things.

## Cancer Moon and Your Personality Traits

## Cancer Moon Strengths

### You are Protective of Others and Yourself

You are usually very protective of your loved ones, your personal feelings, and even your decisions. It almost seems like you are deliberately not telling anyone else about what you are going through, as this is the only way you feel protected without having someone jinxing your luck.

You also worry too much about your loved ones. Being a cardinal sign means that Cancer leads the way to other signs that are soon following you. Think of them as a smaller brother or sister who is always looking up to you.

### You Value Kindness

A Cancer Moon makes you ready to help others whenever they need it. You are sympathetic and kind, and you are always giving, asking nothing in return.

A Cancer Moon is highly sensitive, and often you are aware of others' feelings and struggles.

### You are Curious by Nature

A Cancer Moon usually means that you will go into a room filled with strangers and immediately start investigating who is who, what they do, why they are there, and how he or she can connect with you.

It is like your mind goes to unknown places, trying to decipher what or who is important. This curiosity will also lead you to become explorers of the world—albeit you prefer to explore closer to home, where you still feel part of your comfort zone.

### You are Attentive to Others

A Cancer Moon person does not want "No" for an answer. This is visible when the Moon directs you to continue offering your guests food, beverages, and a fun night. You would like to share everything you have with others just so they feel as lucky as you are.

You value your choices, and you will defend your right to have them even if they are problematic.

## Cancer Moon Weaknesses

### You Keep Things to Yourself

Even if this means others have hurt you, chances are you will never tell the person who hurt you how it makes you feel. A Cancer Moon is someone who prefers to be reserved about his or her genuine feelings, and this, of course, can take a toll on you.

Cancer Moon is used to suppressing emotions. You do so to protect yourself—and others—from going into conflict. Nevertheless, you must remember that communicating with others about how and why you feel a certain way will help the Cancer Moon heal you.

### You are Too Sentimental

A Cancer Moon can feel so many things at the same time. You do not even know where to start and how to manage all those feelings. A Crab Moon knows you need to work on your sentimentality to overcome old inner issues you may have.

Not that a person should not be sentimental, but a Cancer Moon takes this characteristic to extreme levels. You end up being codependent on others, leading you to more frustrations when the other person doesn't behave as the Crab expects them to behave.

### You Think Too Much

Crabs perceive even more. It seems like all your senses are on full display and connect with the external world. You can feel energies from far away. You know when your friends are sad or when strangers are going through a tough time. You can sense others.

As a result, you overthink things concerning other people. You will constantly navigate another person's problems if you think you can offer help or ease them.

### You Get Frustrated Easily

A Crab Moon is the first to get frustrated when something does not go their way. You are still communicating how you feel, and until you reach that point, you will disregard those who are not on the same wavelength as you.

As an individual under this Moon sign, you know that you need to improve your communication skills. Yet, you will still have trouble trying to voice your opinions, especially when it is a new relationship or making new friends.

## Cancer Moon and Your Love Compatibility

The Crab's Moon is someone who values their independence, feels everything, and thinks too much about their lives and their loved ones' lives. Regardless of its Sun or Moon location, this water sign usually has love compatibility with other Air Moon signs (Aquarius, Gemini, Libra) or with Earth Moon signs (Capricorn, Taurus, Virgo).

As a Cancer Moon, you want to share your deepest fears without feeling judged. You look for someone like a Libra, who will bring balance to your life and show you another view of life.

A Cancer Moon needs to see other people's perspectives, or you will be too consumed by your mind. A Libra will bring much-needed air to the Crab–something essential–as it helps water flow.

A Cancer moon is the one that seeks compassion and understanding first when you just meet someone. You are not afraid of embracing your feelings, which means you feel comfortable enough with your true colors.

Yet, a Cancer Moon is less compatible with a Pisces Moon because they are both water signs. Too much water and you can have excessive flooding, and this could be translated as a too intense person who is very passionate but is still trying to figure out who they are. When two water signs are together, it feels as if they become one. They are not even aware of their internal differences anymore because they mirror everything they do and agree with it.

# Cancer as a Sun Sign and the Different Moon Signs

### Cancer Sun + Aries Moon

This combination creates deeply sensitive people who sometimes struggle to know where to direct their strengths. When your Aries Moon appears in Cancer, you are too focused on the details instead of looking at the bigger picture.

You also usually depend on others. This way, you help yourself discover who you are, based on what the other person thinks of you. You do not mind jumping from one feeling to the next, which could bring much frustration or hard times, especially when Aries, a fire sign, continues to push a mellow Cancer.

### Cancer Sun + Taurus Moon

This mix has something very special going on around them. As a result, you are a very grounded individual who looks forward to nurturing and taking care of others. You love the attention, yet it is perfectly fine when the spotlight is on another person.

The earth sign can make your Crab feel like they need to go on exciting adventures all over the world, knowing that they have already built a stable home to come back to shortly.

### Cancer Sun + Gemini Moon

A Crab loves their dependence on others, situations, or feelings. However, if you are in combination with the Twins, chances are your Crab feels propelled to become independent and forge their path. You're not afraid to go deep down to discover your darkest emotions.

Yet, you will also make a point of communicating how you feel because you know your signs can work together to make life easier. It is not just black and white anymore; there are many more colors to choose from.

### Cancer Sun + Cancer Moon

A double Cancer has a constant risk of drowning, despite knowing how to swim. You have so much watery energy that you will feel the need to have more and more water, only for you to go deep down an emotional path.

You feel what others are feeling, and this could bring lots of uncomfortable situations for you. A double Cancer struggles when it is time to say "No" as you are too busy trying to avoid problems.

### Cancer Sun + Leo Moon

A person with this combination is someone more relaxed and with an inner flame hard to water down. You need to feel safe, yet you will also explore new areas outside your comfort zone.

The Crab has a strong shell that slowly burns away whenever Leo is around. This makes you go through many processes that allow you to grow and become stronger than ever.

### Cancer Sun + Virgo Moon

This Cancer is selective about the people who come close to them. You will make sure they know it as well—as you won't accept a new person only because they are friends of a friend. You will try you many times to see if they are worthy of your trust.

But when this Cancer knows their closest friends and family, Virgo makes sure they are protected, nurtured, and loved. This combination makes you revolve around your emotional and social spheres, and you usually do not distinguish between the two.

### Cancer Sun + Libra Moon

The Crab is known for having a mama bear's instinct. Libras are famous for taking care of intimate relationships. As a result, your combination will nurture each other's strengths and partner up to go through your weaknesses. Libra balances out Cancer's powerful emotions, whereas the Crab gives Libra a more intense outlook on life.

You know that there are two sides to a situation, and you will choose both sides so that you can reach a clearer picture. You are emotionally strong yet generous, and you're always looking for others, yet you know your worth.

**Cancer Sun + Scorpio Moon**

This is another intense combination, and you work well together—mainly because of your likeness. But you will still go through challenging moments when the tides rise above their usual levels.

Scorpio is paired with masculine energy, whereas Cancer is a feminine force. You feel it is the right time to show these two energies, so you are straightforward and passionate about the things you love.

**Cancer Sun + Sagittarius Moon**

You are strongly connected to your inner child. The Crab is the family sign, and Sagittarius is the one who loves to play and bring the light wherever they go.

Sometimes people may wonder where you come from because you do not take yourself too seriously. You know that for you to heal past traumas, you must laugh at yourself.

**Cancer Sun + Capricorn Moon**

Cancer is known for being sentimental, whereas Capricorn not only runs away from their emotions, but they are also effusive about their feelings. On the one hand, Capricorn can let your Cancer have a more grounded tone to their emotions. On the other hand, your Crab will show Capricorn a new side of himself or herself, the emotional one.

You are aware of your place in the world. Results stimulate you, and you want to be the best at everything you do. You have an actual sense of legacy and loyalty, especially when you know people look up to you.

### Cancer Sun + Aquarius Moon

Cancer and Aquarius is an independent yet emotionally stable person. This combination makes sure you stay emotionally detached when you feel something may be odd about a situation. Also, you rely on your instinctive nature to make important decisions, and it usually works well in your favor.

Aquarius is an air sign, so Cancer often feels more at ease when you are helping others. This combination is the perfect balance between being of service and staying true to oneself.

### Cancer Sun + Pisces Moon

All double water sign combinations are intense, but this one takes intensity to a whole new level. This combination can translate different energies in seconds. You are almost a psychic when you are born under these two signs.

You are very intuitive, and you need to keep your signs in balance to release old energy carried out by empathic Cancer.

# Chapter 5: Leo Moon

**Symbol:** The Lion

**Element:** Fire

**Quality:** Fixed

**Ruling House:** Fifth

**Ruling Planet:** Sun

## A Brief Explanation of the Moon in Leo

Leo is often considered one of the most intelligent and down-to-earth signs. They are natural leaders and are used to having others following their paths.

Because you have a Leo Moon, you are usually the first to jump into unknown territory, and you will gladly do so with a smile on your face. You are attracted to danger because you are aware of your inner strength.

As a Leo, you love to protect yourself and your loved ones. You are known for your strength, yet your vulnerability is always shown. As expected from a fire sign, Leo, the Lion, roars and spits fire and cannot contain it.

The Lion needs to feel everybody's attention, or they will have a tantrum trying to prove their worth. Then again, you are very loyal, and you will stay with your real friends throughout the most troublesome times without asking questions.

Moreover, if you want to keep active, you must be a Leo. If you want to encourage others and make them feel strong, you have a Moon in Leo. You are the cheerleaders of the Zodiac.

Lions are also known for their dramatic temper, but instead of putting people off with this, more and more individuals are attracted to you.

## Leo Moon and Your Personality Traits

## Leo Moon Strengths

### You are Leaders of the World

A Leo Moon is someone who loves to lead others patiently. Others usually admire you because you represent alternative possibilities since Lions always have an answer.

People feel attracted to a Leo Moon almost immediately because they sense your natural leadership, but also because you genuinely care about others.

### You Have a Lot of Self-confidence

A Lion Moon makes you know yourself so well that even you celebrate your weaknesses. You know you have had to go through that path to become fierce, stronger, and more independent than ever.

Lions are known for their high levels of self-confidence, something they have built throughout their entire lives. If you say you can do something, it is because you are excellent at it. There is no middle way with a Leo Moon.

### You Know Your Value

Alongside having strong self-confidence, a Leo Moon will let you know how valuable you are. You are the ones to get a team moving; after all, you are represented by one of the fastest animals on Earth.

Leo Moon knows how to speak to the world, but they know how to make the world speak to them. Everything you do is based on how valuable that information or situation can be in your life.

### You are Brave Enough to be Admired by Others

Lions are, without a doubt, the bravest sign of the Zodiac. It is second nature to you. You will never freeze in front of danger. On the contrary, you will probably look it straight in the eyes and say, "I was waiting for you."

The Leo Moon also knows when to say sorry and makes you apologize whenever you have hurt another person.

## Leo Moon Weaknesses

### You are a Stubborn Individual

You are the first to admit that you are right, and everyone else is wrong. As a fixed sign, you will also have trouble trying to see beyond your nose. According to you, your ideas deserve attention, and others should pay respect.

As a result, you become fixated and will, stubbornly, defend your ideals until the end. A Leo Moon is usually a person who will fight endlessly. Even if you are mistaken, you will still try to change the other person's mind.

### You Enjoy Fighting Others

Only because you are aware of your strength, you also know that people are afraid of you, so you use this as an advantage and fight aggressively for what you believe in. A Leo Moon is too proud and will continue to fight only because "they had already started fighting in the first place."

You also put yourself above anyone else. It does not mean you think you are better than the rest, but you will make sure everyone knows who is in charge, and when you fight, you get your opponent's admiration.

### You Love the Spotlight

You never seem to get tired of the attention. This could be a weakness, especially when the Leo Moon is too self-centered and starts showing off their knowledge, strength, or ways of being.

It seems like you know the rest of the world has a useless perspective compared to yours. You know it all; hence, why you need to show your knowledge to others. Being in the spotlight is just one way of doing so.

### You are Insecure, and You Hide It

You are good at hiding your insecurity, which is why you will always jump into the spotlight. A Leo Moon may seem like a confident person, and you truly are up to a point, but when a Leo moon does not know something or is completely clueless about a subject, they will make your insecurities run fast.

A Leo moon finds reassurance in others. If someone compliments you, it must mean you are doing something good. If no one ever says anything, you will immediately start thinking something is odd.

## Leo Moon and Your Love Compatibility

The Leo Moon is someone who feels at the top of the world all the time. They are also someone who knows how fast they must run to catch their prey. Regardless of its Sun or Moon location, this sign usually has love compatibility with other Fire Moon signs (Sagittarius, Aries) or Air Moon signs (Aquarius, Gemini, Libra).

A Leo Moon needs someone who can make a fire with them or, at least, spread their flames. They have a lion's strength, and they need a partner who can keep up with their inner drive but never compete against them for the spotlight.

If you have a Leo Moon, you are likely going to fight for your lover's love, even if they have already given you a "No" for an answer. If you cannot be together, Leo Moon will overcome this and make the relationship happen.

A Leo moon is the one that seeks love through your superior sexual position, especially when you are starting a new relationship. You are aware of your sexiness, so to you, it is perfectly acceptable to blend in with someone who is as sensual as you are. Otherwise, your connection will soon fade away. A Leo Moon is very compatible with Gemini, especially when they communicate with each other how they feel and what they want.

A Leo Moon is less compatible with a Cancer Moon. The fire sign will probably want to explore not only the world but also the entire universe if possible. Meanwhile, the water sign is glad to stay at home, exploring their inner self. A Cancer Moon will also probably think Leo is extravagant and someone who does not know how to keep things to themselves. As you already know, the Cancer sign loves their privacy.

## Leo as a Sun Sign and the Different Moon Signs

### Leo Sun + Aries Moon

You are, undoubtedly, a fiery individual. You love to love, but you also love independence more than your relationship with an Aries Moon. Due to this, the Aries Moon will make you stay detached from others.

Nevertheless, you must work hard to establish your relationships with healthy boundaries, or you may be at risk of burning everything down—metaphorically speaking—too soon.

### Leo Sun + Taurus Moon

One minute you are waiting patiently, and the next minute, you are trying to run away from everything. You are always pulling away from two different directions without truly knowing where you need to direct your energies. These are both fixed signs, and this is visible from miles away.

A Taurus Moon is an intensive, stubborn person. This combination makes you someone who tries too hard to forget but cannot do so. Due to this, you always remember who has hurt your feelings.

### Leo Sun + Gemini Moon

You communicate, with explicit details, how you feel about absolutely everything in life. You are also the one to tell others what they need to do, even if they did not ask for your opinion.

You tend to overanalyze everything. You will often struggle with yourself because, on the one hand, you have the Gemini Moon, which tells you that you are intellectually capable of everything. On the other hand, you are the Lion, who is always ready to jump in, regardless of your lack of skills or knowledge.

### Leo Sun + Cancer Moon

This combination can be a struggle from day one. It can be argued that Leo is a very fiery sign, unafraid of damage. Whereas Cancer Moon is somewhat emotional and afraid of many things. One is fire, and the other is water, so every time the fire comes up, the water sign gladly tells it to go back to where it came from.

Still, not everything is negative with your combination, because you are emotionally intelligent when necessary. You are also the ones to love others no matter what, as both signs are open for propagating their love.

### Leo Sun + Leo Moon

Think about how you behave–you are probably a physically, mentally, or spiritually powerful individual who is not afraid to speak your mind. Now, think about a double Leo. You are fire!

A double Leo means you are creative, fierce, courageous, happy, and dramatic. You need to be in constant motion, which is why you will always practice or learn something new. You fill energy levels by going into unknown territories.

### Leo Sun + Virgo Moon

A person with this combination is usually someone capable of sending loving flames to their loved ones, even from a distance. They are the ones who will always make you feel at home, even if you have not seen or spoken to them in years.

As this is your combination, you will wait until you are ready to speak about your feelings. Once you share them, you will do so very dramatically.

### Leo Sun + Libra Moon

Although Leos may not seem like it, they are very romantic individuals who love to have company. You are the social butterflies of the Zodiac–albeit in the Lion version. When you have a Libra Moon, you can also encounter a need to be surrounded by other people.

Sometimes it may seem like you can never be yourself. Even when others are in your presence, you will still crave more company. Nonetheless, it is paramount for you to pay attention to others and sometimes forget about the rest of the world for a minute or two.

### Leo Sun + Scorpio Moon

This person has two very strong yet different signs. A Scorpio Moon is usually someone intense and serious, and Leo is always the soul of the party. The real trick within this combination is never to overshadow the other one.

This combination likes to control things, even if it means that they will go deep down a rabbit hole trying to find answers. You have questions, and you want to discover the truth.

### Leo Sun + Sagittarius Moon

Having a great time is your middle name. It is as simple as that. In all seriousness, you are one of the funniest people on the planet. You love having a good time, and you are not afraid to laugh at yourself.

Leo will always want to keep things simple in their dramatic world, but the word simplicity could differ from one person to the next. Having a Sagittarius Moon will also make you feel calmer because the Archer is less dramatic than its fellow fire sign, Leo.

### Leo Sun + Capricorn Moon

You need to help others. You will immediately drop everything and come to rescue the rest of the world in no time. Leo tends to focus on their relationships, and even though Capricorn is not usually the one to say, "I care about you," they are the ones that will act first.

Having a Capricorn Moon means your Leo will likely focus on their inner self, and their journey is surely going to be a very emotional and intense ride. They will rely on their ability to stand up again, no matter how many times it is needed.

### Leo Sun + Aquarius Moon

These two signs are direct opposites on the Zodiac Chart. They will bring balance to one another, yet they will also push the other to get out of their comfort zone and see beyond their noses.

Having an Aquarius Moon means your Leo is ready to let their emotions disperse for a while. They are not getting emotional all the time—although they may feel like their fire is ready to burst out and spread around thanks to the air sign.

### Leo Sun + Pisces Moon

Leo loves to be at the center of the storm. Fortunately for your fire sign, having a Pisces Moon means that they can bounce to that place, or they can completely disappear underwater.

You have a more mellow personality. You are a highly sensitive individual who empathizes with others. Yet, you still have an internal battle to fight. Who is going to win, water or fire?

# Chapter 6: Virgo Moon

**Symbol**: The Virgin

**Element**: Earth

**Quality**: Mutable

**Ruling House**: Sixth

**Ruling Planet**: Mercury

## A Brief Explanation of the Moon in Virgo

A person with a Virgo Moon is someone who meticulously investigates the finest details in life. They are hard workers—as they are always focusing on their jobs—but they are also the greatest servers of humankind.

A Virgo Moon makes you the family-based individual you thought you would never become. You will ask others to visit you, and you will make them feel part of your family. You will always pay attention to their needs, desires, and lifestyle—although this could mean that you forget about yourself occasionally.

Virgos are the ones that play by the book, so with this Moon, it is impossible to leave things to chance. You want to be behind everything, and if you can make something happen, that is excellent news. Even in the middle of a defeat, you will still say it was a splendid opportunity to learn something new.

However, a Virgo Moon can be tough whenever they need to be. People know not to mess with you, or you will gladly put them on the "list" of people who have wronged you. Yet, a Virgo Moon is often a hopelessly romantic person. You may not be very expressive, but you will show your feelings in your way.

A Virgo Moon is someone who organizes his or her chaos. The term chaos is relative, and Virgos are known for being in the custody of it all. Thus, there is no room for being a chaotic person.

You have strong maternal or paternal instincts, and you will make sure people know how you feel. The planet Mercury—the same planet that rules Gemini—rules Virgo, so it is expected that you love to communicate clearly and concisely as a Virgo Moon.

A Virgo Moon will always look for the not-so-bright side, but this does not mean they are not kind. They are usually very sweet individuals. You love helping others, and you will do everything you can to make sure everyone else is okay.

But this is a mutable sign, so you are always looking into ways of transforming yourself and the situations you are in. A Virgo Moon needs to have control all the time.

# Virgo Moon and Your Personality Traits

## Virgo Moon Strengths

### You Help Everyone You Can

A Virgo Moon cannot stop themselves: when they see someone who needs help, they are the first to offer it or even step in and just do it.

You have a sixth sense where you can feel when another person needs help, and you are there to give that helping hand to them. If it is in your power, a Virgo Moon will always help others.

### You Can Adapt to Different Situations

You will never ask the "Why me?" question. You will acknowledge the situation and swiftly move on from there. A Virgo person can adapt to any shape or form, and you will usually come out stronger than ever.

As a result, it is common to see a Virgo Moon with several jobs or lots of children. You need this "chaos," only because you need to clean the mess that comes after you. Even if you do not like to admit it, you love being in control of everything.

### You Develop Powerful Connections

Virgo Moon is a motherly figure. Think about a grandma who always gives you more lunch, even though you politely refused a thousand times already. Well, regardless of their gender, a Virgo Moon is that grandma. If they take care of you, they will always ask you to eat more, drink more, and sleep more.

As a Virgo Moon, your loved ones and closest friends feel connected with you because you are aware of your motherly or fatherly figure.

### You Can Communicate Effectively

Mercury rules Virgo, so they are going to be proficient speakers. Overall, they are also great communicators and will sometimes go into long monologues about something that catches their attention.

Though, often, as a Virgo Moon, you will have problems communicating what you feel. You will blatantly try to avoid your deepest emotions because you are scared that the other person will not understand them.

## Virgo Moon Weaknesses

### You Overreact About Everything

As a Virgo Moon, you will probably call a tiny snake an Anaconda because, to you, it may have been. You usually overreact about everything that happens in your life. But you do not do this meanly; you do so because you feel very responsible for yourself and others.

Still, difficult situations could undoubtedly be blown up by a Virgo Moon, only because they are too stubborn to calm down and see life as it is.

### You Cannot Rest

A Virgo Moon can be overactive sometimes. You will feel completely tired, yet you will still help others, or clean the house or get a new job.

Moreover, it is not only on a physical level. A Virgo Moon cannot rest their mind, either, since Mercury makes them want to communicate everything all the time. It almost feels like they have an inside narrator who is always saying things to them.

### You Self-Doubt Constantly

Most likely due to your motherly or fatherly instincts, a Virgo Moon continuously asks themselves if what they are doing is worth it or if they are doing a good job. They constantly doubt their abilities and knowledge.

You do not want to make unnecessary mistakes. So, the more you can avoid them, the better– even if it sometimes means you don't get to do things you love, mainly because of your self-doubt.

### You Have Compulsive Behaviors

If a Virgo Moon has to deal with a serious issue, it could be their compulsive behaviors. They are the ones who will stay until late cleaning or clean the whole place twice in a day because they are focusing too much on toxins, dirty areas, and everything in between.

Sometimes you will show a selfish side because you do not care who must move or where they must go if your Virgo Moon reaches its peak point.

## Virgo Moon and Your Love Compatibility

The Virgo Moon is someone who values the place they live in, is always communicating to others their knowledge, and thinks they should control life, one way or another. Regardless of its Sun or Moon location, this earth sign usually has love compatibility with other Water Moon signs (Pisces, Cancer, Scorpio) or Earth Moon signs (Taurus, Capricorn).

As a Virgo Moon, you need someone who can step on common ground with you, help you move toward achieving your goals, and is not afraid to go on a cleaning spree when necessary.

In fact, as a Virgo Moon, you are likely going to clean until the end of the world, as you cannot stand still while your surroundings are a mess. You are so stubborn about this that you won't even mind losing friendships along the way if you stay committed to the truth.

A Virgo Moon seeks comprehension and support. You doubt yourself, so a Pisces person can offer Virgo stability and confidence. This loving couple could go to the Moon and back together, especially when they both allow each other to know each other on deeper levels.

A Virgo moon is less compatible with an Aries Moon. The fire sign will probably want to travel the world or explore new cultures, whereas the Virgo Moon would like to explore their safety zone, regardless of whether Aries likes it.

## Virgo as a Sun Sign and the Different Moon Signs

### Virgo Sun + Aries Moon

If these two signs are combined, chances are they make you forget about yourself most of the time. There could be a constant struggle between the Aries Moon and the Virgo Sun because they cannot stay focused on your personal needs.

Besides, Aries will bring flames to the equation, so your Virgo Sun can become hypocritical to others and yourself. You like being free to choose what you want, but you coerce that freedom to others.

### Virgo Sun + Taurus Moon

You try hard to unfold mysteries and are always reading the small print. By nature, you are the perfect definition of what an earth sign is: you're grounded, happy to serve others, and always work toward your goals.

Taurus will give Virgo the strength to feel their emotions. But sometimes, this process can take a very long time, as both signs tend to drift yet at a steady pace. As a double earth sign, you are grounded, and you are best friends with everyone because they genuinely admire you.

### Virgo Sun + Gemini Moon

Virgo is the mother of the rest of the Zodiac signs, and a Gemini Moon is someone who likes to be mothered. These two combined often struggle with being both independent and relying on others.

You need to communicate how you feel all the time, and you are usually an excellent storyteller, especially when you talk about feelings. Yet, it seems like you still have a long road ahead to allow yourself to feel, instead of describing everything.

### Virgo Sun + Cancer Moon

This Virgo combination is someone who lovingly feels with his or her heart and mind. They have an interesting mix between being very sensitive (thanks to the Crab) and very mental (thanks to the earth sign).

Due to this, you will make sure everyone else feels protected, nurtured, and loved. This combination revolves around your emotional and social spheres, and you rarely distinguish between the two.

### Virgo Sun + Leo Moon

Virgo and Leo are an interesting combination to have, especially because you are an emotional yet very detached person compared to others. If you have this combination, you're okay with walking by yourself because you know how much you can endure.

A Leo Moon is very intense, and you usually send flames flying around wherever you go. Your sense of humor is parched and straightforward, which is a quality admired by many.

### Virgo Sun + Virgo Moon

If you are under this combination, chances are you do not know how to ask for help or to receive it. You struggle with knowing that you cannot do something yet.

However, you are a mutable sign, which means you soon realize this may be all in your head, and you shift your way of thinking. Now you can do everything you set your mind to. You know you are strong, and this strength makes you realize it is okay to sometimes ask for help.

**Virgo Sun + Libra Moon**

If you have this combination, you are likely in a long-term relationship, or you prefer being in a relationship than being single. You want to partner up with someone, travel the world with them, learn new things, and come back to your grounding area.

Venus, the planet of love, rules Libra. This is a great thing for you because your Libra Moon will mellow down your Virgo Sun—the one that makes you quiet when it is time to express your feelings.

**Virgo Sun + Scorpio Moon**

Whether you perceive from others or just for yourself, it seems like you know what is about to happen all the time. Your Virgo Sun takes care of the details, where your Scorpio Moon guides you through your intuitive thinking and knowing.

You are also an intense person, but you can thank your Scorpion Moon for that. If you would like to remain in balance, try to meditate or do another relaxing technique. Ideally, you would want your mind to stop swimming around due to that Scorpio Moon.

**Virgo Sun + Sagittarius Moon**

If someone in Virgo self-identifies as an adventurer, this is going to be you. You are curious by nature, and you love to travel, yet you are always longing for home. Your earth sign will want to take the lead all the time, though it is the Fire Moon that ends up winning the battle most of the time.

If you have this combination, you are likely a very social person. You will want to go to every single party there is or be in all places simultaneously. Going to bed early is not something you do. External beliefs do not limit your independence.

### Virgo Sun + Capricorn Moon

If you have your Moon on this earth sign, chances are you like working hard. You are the one who always has money at the end of the month because you take provisions daily. All your efforts are likely to pay off.

Besides, you also have a strong desire for stability, and your security is not dependable on anyone else. You are your own best friend, which can take you to dark places at some points if you do not work on those weaknesses.

### Virgo Sun + Aquarius Moon

Don't look further for a more cerebral sign combination. You are the one. This does not mean you don't have a heart; it only means that you prefer to think with your head–and sometimes you prefer not to feel at all. Perhaps emotions make you feel uncomfortable, and you avoid those places.

Nevertheless, this is an interesting combination because your Virgo Sun makes you serve others, which you enjoy doing. So, you are constantly asking yourself, "How do I serve others?" and "How can I be by myself?" under this combination.

### Virgo Sun + Pisces Moon

If you look at the Zodiac wheel, Virgo and Pisces are opposite each other. Thanks to this, you have an inner balance that few other signs have. You are in between the inner layers and outer layers constantly. Your earth sign will always tell you how to feel, but your water sign will show you how to feel.

Make sure your Virgo Sun does not dry out your Pisces Moon, or you will lose your creative side, the one that reconnects you to yourself. If you stay calm and integrate these two signs, you will likely feel—and be—happier.

# Chapter 7: Libra Moon

**Symbol**: The Scales

**Element**: Air

**Quality**: Fixed

**Ruling House**: Seventh

**Ruling Planet**: Venus

## A Brief Explanation of the Moon in Libra

If you have a Libra Moon, you are usually an individual who likes to feel raw emotions. As an air sign, you are highly perceptive of your surroundings, and your intellectual capacities are superior to the rest.

Your ideal day is spending time with your loved ones, reconnecting with the energies that help you shape your personality. You love analyzing your feelings, but you can also observe them through an equanimous lens.

If you were born under this sign, you like to focus your energies on others. You are the balance that is needed in the world. Yet, you also depend on others so that they can balance you out.

Unexpectedly, you like working in pairs or groups. You like being social, and when others get to know you, they will soon realize how lucky they are to be connected with you. No wonder they call you the Diplomat–you make everyone feel loved.

You are also diligent and purposely see the beautiful side of life, despite the setbacks you may experience throughout life.

With a Libra Moon, you sometimes feel you are constantly floating around, and it is hard for you to know where you belong. Hence, you always end up breaking rules that may seem unconventional to you–you are the law, so you're the one who chooses what is right and what is wrong.

Your Moon will also guide you toward asking tough questions all the time. You will judge, but only because you perceive more from both sides.

You have an emotional equilibrium that other dual signs would like to have, and even on your worst days, you remain calm and centered.

You love to love others. If you could spend your life loving people, you would. However, you are also a strong-willed individual who has a darker side. You may be codependent on others, precisely because you are still trying to figure out who you are. It is like you're always shifting from one thing to another.

## Libra Moon and Your Personality Traits

## Libra Moon Strengths

### You Know How to Compromise

If a couple is going through a difficult situation, you are the one who usually says, "How can we equally take the burden?" You know you cannot have everything you want in life, yet the more you let go of things, the more other things come back to you.

You are in a constant state of compromise. If family or friends do not know what to choose, you are the one jumping in, reminding them of the pros and cons of their decisions. People will go to you precisely because of this.

### You Listen Carefully and Effectively

When you are communicating with a person, you are doing so attentively. You submerge yourself in what they are telling you, and you will put yourself in their shoes, just to see what it is like from the other side of the room.

Naturally, others realize this, too, and will become more interested in you. A Libra Moon makes everyone feel loved, cared for, and heard.

### You are Very Relaxed

You are not looking for fights, but you know life and its inevitable ways of being, so if an argument arises, you will do your best to remain calm throughout the discussion. Sometimes the other person realizes this and tries to play it against you, but your equanimous energy will see through it.

You do not hold anger against anybody, as you are the only person aware of the value of your energy. You will apologize if you think it is necessary. If not, you will stay true to yourself.

### You Have a Creative Soul

If one thing does not work out, you know there are many other things you can do. You are great at everything you set your mind to, and if you don't know something, you will learn it in no time.

You are hungry for creativity. You are the one who thinks if a person is not creating something, they are not doing anything valuable. This, alongside your curiosity, can take you to faraway places.

# Libra Moon Weaknesses

## You Sabotage Yourself Constantly

You are represented by the Scales. This means that if you are not in a balanced state of mind, you are likely always going back and forth, trying to make your mind up about how you feel.

You sabotage yourself constantly, precisely because you cannot choose. You see under a very negative lens or through a very positive one, and when you see things in different colors, you question if that is possible.

## You Hide Your Inner Self

It is not like you do not want others to know how you are, but you are constantly trying to avoid fights or arguments for the sake of your energy. Yet, it may also be because you don't like others to encounter your darkest side, the one that puts you in touch with everything you need to work on for you to grow.

You also avoid talking about your feelings because you are a very mysterious Moon sign. So, if something does not particularly fit with your agenda, you can always go back to a different hidden place.

## You are Too Nice

Sometimes you can be too naïve, and others take advantage of you. You deeply believe everybody is good until proven otherwise. Subsequently, you are the first to defend others. If you do not do it, who would do it for you?

Being too nice can eventually lead you to have other types of problems, especially in a relationship when the other person is crossing boundaries.

### You Don't Say No

You always say "Yes" to everything and everyone. You are generous, naïve, and rarely answer "No." This may be a serious problem for Libra Moon people, especially when their self-esteem is low.

There is only so much you can give while receiving nothing in return. This can be too hard to bear for Libra Moon individuals, but you need to listen to your intuition and see where it leads you.

## Libra Moon and Your Love Compatibility

The Libra Moon is someone who values the power of having a choice. You are also someone nice, who tries to get along with everyone you meet. Regardless of its Sun or Moon location, this sign usually has love compatibility with other Air Moon signs (Aquarius, Gemini) or Fire Moon signs (Aries, Leo, Sagittarius).

If you have a Libra Moon, you need someone that will help you decide. Sometimes you even need a person who will take the lead and decide for you. This will take the weight off your shoulders. A great match would be an Aquarius person because they are very determined in what they want to achieve.

Your Libra Moon is likely going to wonder if that person is the right one for you. You are stubborn about this, but only because you do not want to disappoint yourself again. You don't enjoy going through those emotions.

A Libra Moon is the one that seeks equal pleasure, especially when a relationship is at an early stage. You are not afraid of exploring all different sides, nor the other person.

Conversely, a Libra Moon is less compatible with an Earth Moon. The air sign will probably want to feel relaxed, and the earth sign, such as Capricorn, will constantly remind you to choose a side.

# Libra as a Sun Sign and the Different Moon Signs

### Libra Sun + Aries Moon

If you have this combination, you sometimes feel you are the soul of the party, but the next minute, you feel you want to go home and cuddle your pets. Your Libra Sun will tell you to partner up, and your fire sign is always telling you to go by yourself.

An Aries Moon is likely making you feel you have an inner flame that needs to burst out, and you would like to do so in solitude, something Libra is not completely used to.

### Libra Sun + Taurus Moon

If this is your combination, surely you feel deep oceans of love within yourself. This occurs because Venus, the planet of Love, rules both signs. You have great energy, but sometimes it can be too clingy for some.

As Taurus Moon is an earth sign, your air sign will be kept on the ground. You know how to love wisely and are very loyal to those closest to you.

### Libra Sun + Gemini Moon

You have double air signs; you represent the Twins and the Scales. You love to chat, are highly intelligent, and tend to speak your mind unfiltered.

As a result, your Gemini Moon makes you feel you always have great ideas, and your Libra Sun is the one that calms you down before you get too excited about endless possibilities.

### Libra Sun + Cancer Moon

Your Crab Moon will want to surround everyone with love, as that sign is known for having a parenthood vibe. Libras are also known for caring for their loved ones. If you have these two signs, you are likely a devout individual. You pour yourself into helping others who may struggle.

Your Libra Sun will balance your Cancer's powerful emotions, whereas the Crab gives Libra a more intense outlook on life. Be careful, though, as you may become too dependent on others.

### Libra Sun + Leo Moon

Your Leo Moon will scream at your Libra Sun to continue searching for love, as both sides are known for their romantic ways. This combination means you are the life of the party, and you enjoy it.

Sometimes it may seem like you can never be your true self, especially when you feel others shine brighter than you. Keep in mind that you must pay attention to what your intuition tells you since she is the one to call the shots.

### Libra Sun + Virgo Moon

You are a person who loves being in a relationship. You may seem detached at first, but as soon as you explore your depths, you realize that being with another person truly makes you happy. Now, you will still need to work on your hypercritical ways, considering not everyone is ready to hear everything you have to say.

You usually take your time to trust others, and it is perfectly normal for you to test others before you trust them completely. Even if you already know the person and they are your best friend, you still have some trouble issues you need to bring light on.

### Libra Sun + Libra Moon

There are never enough double Libras in the world. If you are a double Libra, chances are you like being with others, but you do not enjoy discussing your emotions. You are more concerned about living peacefully rather than navigating through the seas of feelings.

But you will need to find a healthy balance. You need to come to terms with the fact that you will always have too many choices to choose from, and this could take you out of your comfort zone.

### Libra Sun + Scorpio Moon

You are usually the person who tries to bring calm and peace to your friends' and family's lives. You are the one who will try to go to the bottom of the ocean if that means you will find the truth, and you will honor it.

You love speaking out in public because you know you are diplomatic and can get things done. Still, you need to keep some things for yourself, especially when you don't feel too comfortable around others.

### Libra Sun + Sagittarius Moon

You are the most optimistic person ever. You're one of few who will continuously get up and fight for their rights–lovingly fight, that is, because you avoid confrontations.

You also love adventures and trying to see the good in everything. You are the perfect travel companion for so many people, and you're not even aware of it. If you have this combination, you probably never say "No" to something spontaneous, such as traveling on your bicycle through South America or living on an almost deserted island for a couple of months.

**Libra Sun + Capricorn Moon**

If you have these signs, you are likely to work on your dreams. You're the one who always has a new project coming up or continuously working on great, creative ideas. Your sun in Libra will soften your Capricorn Moon, which is great for you. Otherwise, you may be too secluded from the rest of the world.

There is unique energy within you because, on the one hand, you feel confident about yourself and your connection to others. On the other hand, you are completely focused on what will happen next and what you can achieve.

**Libra Sun + Aquarius Moon**

If you are a mixture of these two signs, you should know that everything changes, and everything passes. You may feel confused throughout your life because these two signs are known for their wandering abilities.

You should know that you are an integral person trying to see the good in the world and are working toward achieving it. It is perfectly fine if you feel like one day you can save the rest of humanity, and your Libra Sun will help you do that.

**Libra Sun + Pisces Moon**

If you were born with this combination, you have most likely experienced difficult phases throughout life. First, you want to swim deep into the ocean of your thoughts. Then, you decide it is best to stay aloof, somewhere where you can see all sides.

You also have an intense emotional intuition, and you need to pay attention to it. You do not accept mistreatments or people who judge others.

# Chapter 8: Scorpio Moon

**Symbol:** The Scorpion

**Element:** Water

**Quality:** Fixed

**Ruling House:** Eighth

**Ruling Planet:** Pluto

## A Brief Explanation of the Moon in Scorpio

If you are a Scorpio Moon, you love to experience new beginnings. You're always looking for that inner drive to explore the rest of the world in seconds. You're a person who only follows your desires and dreams.

If you were born with a Moon in Scorpio, you see things in black and white. Sometimes you may add a splash of color, but you are heading toward some dark area most of the time.

This does not mean you are a bad person or focus too much on negative energies; it just means that you're in touch with death and not afraid of it. You have seen beyond what other signs may have seen and discovered some great mysteries that many would love to find out.

You tend to guard your personal life as if you were a bulldog protecting your owner. But you are also a very loving person once you allow yourself to be with those who love you.

You are highly intelligent and work on difficult projects that require your attention for long periods. However, contrary to popular beliefs, you're an intuitive person who likes to express your feelings with those closest to you. You do not like small chats.

## Scorpio Moon and Your Personality Traits

### Scorpio Moon Strengths

#### You Work Hard

You know that your hard work will pay off eventually, so you give your all to become the best at what you do.

You are the one who is behind many international enterprises, and your boss knows how dependable they are on you because no one will ever do the job as you do.

#### You are a Committed Person

Whether you commit yourself to your job, family, or relationships, you will usually put them first. You will even neglect your personal needs to take care of those closest to you.

If your Moon is in Scorpio, you are always looking out for your public image. Not because of vanity, but because you know others are interested in copying you because they think you're a good example.

#### You are Courageous

If you are an artist, everybody is likely talking about your pieces because you dare to speak about things that are considered taboo. You're very creative, and you know that you can speak your mind through your art.

However, you also courageously accept when others show you a new piece of information, even if that destroys your values. Your Scorpio Moon sign will guide you to your truth.

### You are Very Emotional

Although most people will disagree because they do not know you, you are a very emotional individual if your Moon is in Scorpio. You may even have trouble admitting it because you don't want to present yourself in this light.

But you are the one who will scan through others' feelings and energies to see where they come from. Your intuition will also allow you to be certain most of the time.

## Scorpio Moon Weaknesses

### You are Too Rigid

Nobody will ever tell you that you are rigid because they are probably afraid to lose you. This only shows how you see everything one way or another.

Some individuals with a Moon in Scorpio will become obsessed with one thing, and then they will not make time for the rest of their interests. If you just discovered something that fascinated you, chances are you are going to master it in no time.

### You are Manipulative

You know how to get to others' weak points and are not ashamed to admit it. This may be your darker side coming out and trying to express your genuine emotions.

You tend to be manipulative when you sense things are about to change abruptly or want to keep the status quo as it is.

### You Seek Solitude

A Scorpio Moon will gladly stay alone for the entire year. They do not mind not socializing or going out; quite the opposite–staying in is their favorite activity.

However, if you continuously seek solitude, how are you going to grow? You need to let others in, just like they are letting you into their lives.

### Your Insecurities Could Surpass You

You think you are a confident person, and, overall, you are. On the other hand, there may be times when you go deep down within your energies, and you realize that things do not always look good.

Your insecurities are there, and now and then, you allow them to come to the surface to explore. Most of the time, you don't deal with these problems because you are too busy doing something else.

## Scorpio Moon and Your Love Compatibility

The Scorpio Moon is courageous and wants to dive deep into their emotions, yet values their privacy like nothing else. Regardless of its Sun or Moon location, this sign usually has love compatibility with other Air Moon Signs (Aquarius, Gemini, Libra) or Water Moon signs (Pisces, Cancer).

A Scorpio Moon needs someone who can take the plunge with them and who is not afraid to be dark and bring light at the same time. You have very strong values, and you don't take love for granted.

Your Scorpio Moon is likely going to push to the limits. You will truly see who you are once you accept this sign and its effect on your overall life.

A Scorpio Moon seeks stability in a partner. In many ways, a Cancer Moon can share a lot of these feelings with you. But they also emphasize their sexual chemistry first, especially when they are starting new love relationships. A Scorpio Moon is someone willing to go to the next level if that means they will get immediate satisfaction.

Conversely, a Scorpio Moon is less compatible with a Capricorn Moon. The earth sign will tell the Scorpio Moon how they need to behave, which is something the Scorpion cannot tolerate.

## Scorpio as a Sun Sign and the Different Moon Signs

### Scorpio Sun + Aries Moon

If you have this combination, then you are someone who loves to explore your sexual side—and unlike any other Zodiac sign. It should not surprise you if you think that you only attract people so that you can enjoy a steamy night or two.

If this is your combination, you rely on your intuition on every single level. Still, you need to explore the world and see what it is like out there. If not, you are too focused on yourself, and you lose sight of what matters to you—your freedom.

### Scorpio Sun + Taurus Moon

If you have this Moon, you are someone who feels everything profoundly. Your intensity levels are too high most of the time. You have a stubborn Taurus Moon who is constantly telling you what to do.

As a water sign, Scorpio will make Taurus run out of their comfort zone, which is the only way you can grow. What is more, Taurus will bring a sense of emotional stability to your Scorpio Sun, so they become a powerful combination.

### Scorpio Sun + Gemini Moon

This combination is all about following their intuition. Sometimes these two signs will compete to see which one gets your attention the most. The water sign brings a nice intellectual touch to your Gemini Moon, who is always looking for new ideas.

You know how to set boundaries—yet you are always trying to break them—you are not afraid to speak your mind, and you do not have problems telling others to keep quiet if they don't agree with you.

**Scorpio Sun + Cancer Moon**

These two are another intense combination. Although these signs may work well together—mainly because of their likeness—they will still go through challenging moments when the tides rise above their usual levels.

On the other hand, your Scorpio Sun tends to be a very masculine energy, whereas your Cancer Moon has a complete female prowess. If you were born under this combination, you know perfectly well when it is the right time to release these two water signs of existence.

**Scorpio Sun + Leo Moon**

You have two very different, strong, and robust signs knocking at your door. A Scorpio Sun is usually someone intense and serious. Meanwhile, Leo Moon is always the soul of the party. The real trick within this combination is never to overshadow the other one.

You like to control things, even if it means that you will end up going to dark places you never knew existed.

**Scorpio Sun + Virgo Moon**

It seems like you know what is about to happen all the time. Your Virgo Moon is the one that takes care of the bigger picture, whereas your Scorpio Sun will tell you where you need to look at next.

You are also an intensively intuitive person, but you can thank your Scorpion Sun for that. If you would like to remain in balance, try to meditate or do another relaxing technique. Ideally, you would want your mind to stop analyzing everything due to that Virgo Moon.

### Scorpio Sun + Libra Moon

You are usually the person who tries to bring calm and peace to your friends' and family's lives. Although you also warn them, you will show them the reality and truth, and not a blurry ideal.

You love speaking out in public because you know you are diplomatic and can get things done. This is where your Libra Moon comes in. Still, you need to keep some things for yourself, especially when you do not feel too comfortable around others. You don't want to be called rude all the time, especially when others are not ready to understand what you are saying.

### Scorpio Sun + Scorpio Moon

A double Scorpio is a powerful combination. You are probably going through tough times–at least to you, they are very often–because you cannot seem to come to the surface for pure air.

You need to focus your energy on doing something new, which you had never considered before. You need to clean your inner self if you would like to stop struggling with life. You know that you have a lot of potential, but you need to believe in yourself first.

### Scorpio Sun + Sagittarius Moon

You probably debate everything. A simple question, such as "What's for dinner?" can make you dive into rocky areas you never knew you had. A Sagittarius Moon will only intensify these feelings of questioning absolutely everything in life.

You also tend to be a person who likes to run away. It does not matter where you go if you leave the place that makes you feel uncomfortable.

### Scorpio Sun + Capricorn Moon

This combination is powerful, mainly because they differ completely from one another. You probably think that one side of you comes from one planet, and the other one comes from a different universe. The truth is, you are probably right.

You will have to deal with many internal battles to see who comes alive in you. Is the water sign winning? Or did your Capricorn Moon lead the way? Either way, know that everything passes, and soon enough, you will feel like these two signs balance each other in a relatively calm manner.

**Scorpio Sun + Aquarius Moon**

This is a cool and interesting combination. A Scorpio Sun is the one that goes first because they know what they must do. The Aquarius Moon is the one that guides the rest because of his or her ability to perceive how much help everybody else needs.

You are a compassionate person who is not afraid. Nothing can stop you, and you know you are a valuable resource for many individuals who look up to you. The further you go away from home, the more at peace you feel.

**Scorpio Sun + Pisces Moon**

Both Scorpio and Pisces will fight to keep the throne. Your Pisces Moon is likely telling you to stop swimming in Scorpio's direction. Likewise, your Scorpio Sun is probably telling you that you need to go back to where Scorpio is.

You are always improving yourself. Whether this means you are succeeding academically or inventing new things, your mind travels to alternative places no one else has ever been.

# Chapter 9: Sagittarius Moon

**Symbol:** The Centaur / The Archer

**Element:** Fire

**Quality:** Mutable

**Ruling House:** Ninth

**Ruling Planet:** Jupiter

## A Brief Explanation of the Moon in Sagittarius

You are the independent Moon, the one that can save the rest of the signs, and the one that shows how fun it is to play and continue going further.

You have such a powerful Moon, yet you do not seem to be fully aware of it. With this sign on your Moon, you can travel to faraway places without even leaving your sofa.

You are a natural-born leader supported by Jupiter, the planet of expansion and good luck. No wonder why you always feel as if good luck thunder hit you.

With a Moon in Sagittarius, you were born to be unique. You are the one who goes to the farthest of places only to realize that your true home is within. You idolize foreign cultures, and you are fascinated by how people's minds work, like how you tend to study every phenomenon you see or experience.

You are kind and generous, but you also stick to your truth, and you will let no one get to you. This, of course, could cause you some problems, especially when others think you are just obnoxious. Behind the facade, you are a good friend, one that makes everyone laugh at his or her occurrences.

If you were born with a Moon in Sagittarius, you think fast and act faster. You are a true Zodiac animal and a complete human being.

# Sagittarius Moon and Your Personality Traits

## Sagittarius Moon Strengths

### You are Intelligent

It is not like you give a smart answer; it's more like your whole life is based on providing intelligent answers to people. Everyone comes to you for knowledge and your wise energy.

It is not surprising to see you teaching others, even on your free days. You love helping others, especially for deep philosophical topics that can lead to many sound answers.

### You Care About Others

You may say you don't, but you care more about others than yourself. According to your views, it is okay to help others first, and then the universe will gladly help you too.

Some will argue your reasons, but the truth is, you help others because you care about them. Whether you just met them five minutes ago and you have an instant connection, or if it's someone you know for the last couple of years, it doesn't matter because you would still save both of their lives in a heartbeat.

### You are Quick to Analyze

You are quick to analyze a situation, especially difficult ones. You are a fire symbol, so you will defend your rights until the end.

You are a deep thinker; however, you must take care of yourself and stop analyzing continuously, or you may experience burnout because your mind doesn't ever seem to stop working.

### You are Very Optimistic

A Sagittarius Moon is the most optimistic sign in the Zodiac. Perhaps it is because Jupiter, the biggest and most prominent planet in the galaxy, rules you. Or perhaps it is because you are deeply connected to your true self-vibration. It does not matter. If you visualize something, you get that something.

Being optimistic doesn't mean you are a lucky person all the time. Furthermore, you can–and must–have your off days. But the sign will teach you that a big lesson is to recognize your good thanks to your bad.

## Sagittarius Moon Weaknesses

### You are Too Raw

You do not mind being raw as you cannot be any other way. You are usually the one who will always say the most difficult phrases in a group. You give answers, but you give them in such a straight, raw, and powerful manner that few people are ready to listen to you.

You are brutally honest when you must, even if it is when you are talking to yourself. Sometimes the way you express your feelings could hurt those closest to you.

### You Have No Patience

You are impatient for no reason because most of the time, you end up waiting anyway. Ideally, you would like to do everything in one day. But there are only twenty-four hours in a day, and you must wait sometimes.

You also never slow down, not even for a second. A Sagittarius Moon is constantly trying to spark a fire, even if it is pouring rain outside.

### You are an Attention Seeker

More often than you would like to admit, you have seen yourself trying to catch everybody's attention. It is like you feed yourself through that. You do not know what it is, but having their attention makes you feel you have power and control the situation.

You claim attention, but you don't give it yourself. Most of the time, you get lost when trying to hold a conversation with others. It is not because they are not exciting; it's because you get bored easily, especially when the attention is on others.

### You Seem Careless

Others can perceive you as careless when they argue with you. It is almost as if you don't mind what the other person thinks or feels, as you need to get your point across, and you don't mind if you say some hurtful truths.

According to you, you are a hero for speaking out. However, others may disagree with this and consider you rude and careless.

## Sagittarius Moon and Your Love Compatibility

A Sagittarius Moon enjoys being independent and only establishes a relationship with someone else who is as independent and free as they are.

If this is your Moon, chances are you want to live your life eccentrically. Regardless of its Sun or Moon location, this sign usually has love compatibility with other Fire Moon signs (Aries, Leo) or Air Moon signs (Aquarius, Gemini, Libra).

A Sagittarius Moon needs someone who will whisk them away to a different country, or at least to a small village in the middle of nowhere. You want to explore the world, and you want to do so now. You know that if you postpone your dreams, it may be too late at the end of the day.

A Sagittarius Moon is the one that seeks freedom, novelty, and love. You are usually the one that says, "I love you" first, but only because Jupiter rules you, the planet that loves to expand. Your Moon goes especially well with a Gemini, as both of you will try new and fun ways of getting to know each other.

However, a Sagittarius Moon is less compatible with a Capricorn Moon. The fire sign will probably want to travel without ever stopping, whereas the earth sign would like to stay still and build an empire where they are.

# Sagittarius as a Sun Sign and the Different Moon Signs

### Sagittarius Sun + Aries Moon

If you have this combination, you are someone who loves to explore foreign cultures. If it were up to you, you would live in every country in the world throughout your life because you know there is much to see.

You are someone who aims for more. Whether that means learning a new language or taking a risky job, you need to live your life your way. The more you step out of conventional beliefs, the freer you will feel.

### Sagittarius Sun + Taurus Moon

This combination is known to be adventurous, down-to-earth, and terrific storytellers. If your Moon is in Taurus, you are someone who needs to ground constantly. You are not looking at the sky; you are looking at your steps and how far you have come.

However, one sign will try to impose their ways of seeing life onto the other sign. As a result, there is a real possibility of having a persistent inner struggle, seeing as they will both fight hard no matter what.

### Sagittarius Sun + Gemini Moon

If you have ever met a Sagittarius Sun with a Gemini Moon, you know they are up for a laugh. So, if these are your signs, lucky you.

A person with this combination always has something to say, and it is usually something interesting. Your optimistic levels are sometimes over the roof, and you will try your best to achieve your dreams—and often, you're very lucky.

**Sagittarius Sun + Cancer Moon**

A person with this combination is someone who gets along well with children because it strongly connects them with their inner child. Sagittarius will light up even the darkest rooms, whereas the Crab will protect everyone else.

If this is your combination, you don't take yourself seriously, but you take others seriously. You are the soul of any party, but you are also okay with someone else being in the spotlight.

**Sagittarius Sun + Leo Moon**

This is a fun combination. You are a very extroverted person who loves making new friends. Everybody around your neighborhood knows about you and your flamboyant style.

Although your Leo Moon will try to keep things simple, you are a true Sagittarius who loves to show off how much fun you are having. It could be a constant battle between your two sign's egos.

**Sagittarius Sun + Virgo Moon**

If a Sagittarius wants to prove their adventurous side, this combination will be the one. You were born to explore and love traveling, yet you want to build your own home nearby your loved ones.

If you have this combination, you are likely a very social person. You will want to go to every single party there is and be in all places at the same time. Going to bed early is not something you do. External rules do not limit your independence.

**Sagittarius Sun + Libra Moon**

You are an optimistic person, but sometimes your Libra Moon will tell you to please calm down before you cause a big scene. You may have won the lottery, and your Libra Moon will still tell you to chill.

You also love adventures and trying to see the good in everything. However, your Sagittarius Sun goes faster than your Libra Moon, and sometimes, this could mean that you spontaneously travel to the other side of the world over dinner.

**Sagittarius Sun + Scorpio Moon**

You probably have an inner voice that does everything with you and talks with you all the time. That voice is your Scorpio Moon. Even the simplest of questions will be followed by a very long monologue that will explain to your Sagittarius Sun why the Scorpio Moon is right.

You will also intensify your Scorpio Moon because you are one of the biggest fire signs. You will say things in a clear yet concise manner.

**Sagittarius Sun + Sagittarius Moon**

A double Sagittarius Moon is a powerful duo. You are usually the one who always answers "Yes" even when the question isn't over yet. You hear the word "travel" and already have your bags packed and are ready to go.

You cannot stay in one place. It is physically impossible for you. That is why you have probably traveled all year long. You don't mind missing your family or close friends. You know that the rest of the world and people you haven't met are your future family and friends.

**Sagittarius Sun + Capricorn Moon**

This is a complicated and intense combination. A Capricorn Moon is always telling you that you need to do things differently. It also questions everything you are doing and whom you're doing it with.

On the other hand, your Sagittarius Sun is likely telling you they do not care about the Capricorn Moon. However, deep down, you know you limit yourself precisely because of this earth sign. It is time to let go.

### Sagittarius Sun + Aquarius Moon

This is a lovely combination, which is always willing to work hard to experience the life they deserve. A Sagittarius Sun is someone who loves to help, and an Aquarius Moon is the one who needs to help others. Overall, you are a person who is very keen on making yourself feel useful.

You will not sit still for long periods. You're very independent, and you know how much your freedom is valued because you don't know anyone else who thinks or acts like you.

### Sagittarius Sun + Pisces Moon

A Pisces Moon is the one that will make your Sagittarius Sun feel more at peace. The water sign is always looking out for you. Your Moon will water down your Sagittarius's fire when necessary, whether you like it or not.

But your Pisces Moon is also someone who goes deep within. So, you are constantly wondering whether you should continue with your inner philosophical journey.

# Chapter 10: Capricorn Moon

**Symbol:** The Sea-Goat

**Element:** Earth

**Quality:** Cardinal

**Ruling House:** Tenth

**Ruling Planet:** Saturn

## A Brief Explanation of the Moon in Capricorn

If your Moon is in Capricorn, you are someone who loves to work hard and will not stop until you succeed in life. You are happier when working in an office, and you don't mind working more than what you had planned if someone else is noticing your effort.

You are determined and ambitious, and your sign's energy is always propelling you. Your Moon is the one that shows what life is all about. It also shows you your biggest project, which is how you can live life to the fullest, without succumbing to tempestuous behaviors and thoughts.

You love building things, and that includes your life. You overcome many past obstacles and shine lighter when you finally exit that tunnel.

A Capricorn Moon is someone practical. If this is you, you are not afraid to get your hands dirty if necessary—although you would rather have someone else do the dirty job.

A Capricorn Moon is a traditional Moon. In other words, you do not enjoy impressing someone. You are as you are, and if other people can appreciate that, great. If not, they know the door is always open, and they can easily choose to go.

Finally, with a Capricorn Moon, you know your worth. You are your biggest fan, and you're loyal to yourself and those you love.

# Capricorn Moon and Your Personality Traits

## Capricorn Moon Strengths

### You are Fun to be Around

Everybody loves being your friend because you say the funniest things. Sometimes people around you cannot believe you have just said something because you dared to do so, even if they didn't.

You are the soul of the party, and everybody knows and loves your sense of humor. You like being around others, mainly because your Capricorn Moon guides you toward others.

### You are Down to Earth

You are not afraid to admit when you have done something wrong. You don't avoid apologies, because you know you can grow through them. As an earth sign, your feet are constantly on the floor. Due to that, you are a grounded individual who loves sharing their life with others.

You have a strong will and remain connected with those you truly want in your life. The rest can come and go, but you will stay.

### You are Very Loyal

When you love or admire a person, you will always have their back because you know what it is like to suffer alone. You are there for the rest, and you're loyal to them.

You expect others to do the same, but you know everyone is walking a different path. A Capricorn Moon makes you understand this.

### You Follow Your Instincts

You know your instincts guide your life, especially when you focus on a special project or jumping into a new venture.

You know how to reinvent yourself and stay ahead of others. Your charisma is always on display because you follow your instincts.

## Capricorn Moon Weaknesses

### You are Too Strong

You are a tough individual. You do not mind being strong to others or yourself. You know that if a person wants to succeed in life, they need to listen to some hard realities. Yet sometimes you don't measure yourself, and you end up hurting others.

When you are angry, the rest of the world should run away from you. You become a Godzilla because how can the other person not know that what they are doing bothers you?

### You Won't Take "No" for an Answer

You will not stop until the other person tells you "Yes." This could be very annoying to some, but it is one of your biggest traits according to you. Sometimes you will communicate how you feel, whereas other times, you will stay quiet and let your looks talk.

You especially hate it when someone tells you "No" without reason. However, you must understand that sometimes life has bigger plans for you. Not every "No" answer is negative.

### You Cannot Stop Working

You are probably going to bed thinking about what your day will look like the following morning. You are constantly working, even when on vacation. You feel as if you are the most important person in the world, and your business or job will crumble if you're not there.

You tend to forget how to enjoy yourself. Whether it means going out for a meal or seeing your family or friends, you need to have some "you" time; otherwise, your energy levels could be affected.

### You Like to Manipulate Others

You know you can change someone's perception by saying a comment or dropping a hint. You are too emotional, so when you do not like what the other person might do, you will hide your feelings and manipulate them.

This attitude usually gives you problems, but you look at them and go the other way around.

## Capricorn Moon and Your Love Compatibility

The Capricorn Moon is someone who values their safety, comfort zone, and life. If this is your Moon sign, you know that no one will ever be able to stop you from achieving your future when you start visualizing it. Regardless of its Sun or Moon location, this sign usually has love compatibility with other Earth Moon signs (Taurus, Virgo) or Air Moon signs (Aquarius, Gemini, Libra).

A Capricorn Moon needs someone with whom they can feel safe. If you were born under this Moon sign, you are a very curious person, yet you are scared to go by yourself. Think of a person afraid of the dark. They love to sleep but have to sleep with the lights on, or they won't enjoy their rest.

If your Moon is in Capricorn Moon, you are likely telling everyone what you think or believe. If the person does not want to hear it, you will scream it at them because you need to get it off your chest. A Capricorn Moon is compatible with a Pisces Moon because the Fish can calm a Capricorn.

In contrast, a Capricorn Moon is less compatible with a Gemini Moon, even though a Capricorn can get along very well with another air sign, such as Libra. The earth sign is probably too busy trying to explain to the Twins why they shouldn't behave in such a way–which, of course, the Gemini Moon finds annoying.

## Capricorn as a Sun Sign and the Different Moon Signs

### Capricorn Sun + Aries Moon

This combination could present some setbacks, mainly because there is always a struggle between Aries not being consistent and Capricorn trying to be steady with everything they do. As a result, an Aries Moon can make a Capricorn drop everything they are doing.

Because of Capricorn's nonstop desire to succeed and make a name for him or herself, they would cause Aries's intensity to skyrocket.

### Capricorn Sun + Taurus Moon

If you were born with this combination, you are probably the cool boss around. A Taurus Moon will make you work extra hard, and a Capricorn Sun will likely accept this verdict.

A person under these signs is usually someone completely focused on their career and social status. They may have problems trying to navigate their emotions, so it is advisable to try to explore their feelings.

**Capricorn Sun + Gemini Moon**

A Gemini Moon means you love no matter what. A Capricorn Sun means you are having trouble loving others unconditionally, but you are still trying.

Nevertheless, this earth sign will allow the Twins to feel more connected with the world, and the other way around occurs. The Capricorn Sun will make your Gemini Moon feel more connected to the earth.

**Capricorn Sun + Cancer Moon**

Cancer is known for being sentimental, but Capricorn not only runs away from their emotions, but they are also effusive about their feelings. A Cancer Moon means you are likely extra sentimental, and most of the time, it is without you wanting it to be that way.

Results stimulate you, and you want to be the best at everything. You have a genuine sense of legacy and loyalty, especially when you know people look up to you.

**Capricorn Sun + Leo Moon**

If you need someone to help you, call this Capricorn. They will immediately drop everything off and come rescue you in no time. A Leo Moon knows the value of friendships, and they will make you do everything you can to keep those friends around.

Having a Leo Moon means this Capricorn is likely going to focus on their inner self, and their journey is surely going to be a very emotional and intense ride. They will rely on their ability to stand up again, no matter how many times it is needed.

### Capricorn Sun + Virgo Moon

If you have your Moon in this earth sign, chances are you like to work hard and meticulously. You are the one who always has money at the end of the month because you take provisions daily. All your efforts are likely to pay off.

You also have a strong desire for stability, and your security is not dependable on anyone else. Your Virgo Moon will make sure everyone knows how hard you have worked.

### Capricorn Sun + Libra Moon

You are the one who always has a new project coming up or are continuously working on great, creative ideas. Your Capricorn Sun will make you analyze everything before you commit to something.

There is unique energy within you because, on the one hand, you feel confident about yourself and your connection with others. On the other hand, you are completely focused on what is going to happen next and what you can achieve.

### Capricorn Sun + Scorpio Moon

This combination is a powerful one, mainly because they differ completely from one another. You probably think that one side of you comes from one planet, and the other one comes from a different universe. The truth is, you are probably right.

You will have to deal with many internal battles to see who comes alive in you. Is the water sign winning? Or did your Capricorn Sun lead the way? Either way, know that everything passes, and soon enough, you will feel like these two signs match each other in a relatively calm manner.

### Capricorn Sun + Sagittarius Moon

This is a complicated and intense combination. A Capricorn Sun tends to overanalyze everything, and a Sagittarius Moon could not care less. A Capricorn Sun tries to connect with their Sagittarius Moon, but sometimes it feels impossible to do so.

Your Sagittarius Moon is likely telling you they don't care about the Capricorn Sun. However, deep down, you know your fire sign is only trying to make some problems.

**Capricorn Sun + Capricorn Moon**

If you are looking for a forever strengthening sign, look no further. A double Capricorn is a stubborn person, but they will also be the first ones to admit they were wrong.

A double earth sign is likely going to exhaust some people. They are known for being book nerds who need to write everything down, or they won't remember it.

**Capricorn Sun + Aquarius Moon**

This combination is a powerful one because they get along very well. This Aquarius Moon brings a perfect balance to the Capricorn Sun. This Aquarius air sign will teach the Capricorn earth sign how to flow more intensively.

An Aquarius Moon will give you a broader sense of belonging, and you will soon start noticing that there is more to life than your house or backyard.

**Capricorn Sun + Pisces Moon**

These two signs make a lovely combination. Surprisingly, your Pisces Moon will make you go deeper within yourself on a healing journey. It was something you never thought would happen, but it will come to you if you allow it.

You are the one who likes to talk with family and friends for hours, nonstop. They admire you, and you are their leader, sometimes without even knowing it.

# Chapter 11: Aquarius Moon

**Symbol:** The Water Bearer

**Element:** Air

**Quality:** Fixed

**Ruling House:** Eleventh

**Ruling Planet:** Uranus

## A Brief Explanation of the Moon in Aquarius

If a sign represents freedom, Aquarius would be a perfect choice. You are the one who is always fighting for their rights. You are a person trying to achieve your dreams, no matter how big they may seem.

You may come across as an angry person to the external world, but you are a soft teddy bear looking for love. You work well in a team, even if you sometimes don't want to admit it.

If you are born under this Moon Sign, you love to travel to new places, but you also appreciate a still life that you can share with those closest to you.

You do not mind being the "weird one" or the one that stands out. On the contrary, you prefer to differentiate yourself from the rest of the common crowd.

You are very moody, but most people will agree that you have a reason behind your rapid change of moods. You are also anxious about your future—although you tend to forget about it soon afterward.

You love to escape, not necessarily because you may have problems but because you want others to think you are a mysterious person. You are eccentric, and not a single soul would doubt that.

You will also speak your mind, even if it gets you a couple of enemies. You will show your vision of what the world should look like, but you will do so respectfully.

# Aquarius Moon and Your Personality Traits

## Aquarius Moon Strengths

### You are Independent

You like to set your rhythm, and you do not mind others following you. However, if they get in your way, you will kindly tell them where they can go. You are so independent that sometimes, you forget you have family and friends.

You are always looking into ways of becoming independent. Whether you are searching for your career path or would like to be a stay-at-home parent, you're the only one who will have a saying in what you end up doing.

### You Bring Something New to the Table

Everyone who knows you will know this, and they love you because of it. You are usually the one who has new ideas, projects, and goals. You know how to achieve them, and you will work hard to do so.

You are an original person. You're creative and always have something to say that will add value to the conversation.

### You Know How to Innovate

If you were born with an Aquarius Moon, you probably have a successful business or are on your way to creating one. You are a highly innovative person who always strives for the best.

You like to educate yourself to feel like you can educate and help others. Your bosses tend to be happy with you because they know you are a reliable person.

### You are Intelligent

You can read others as if you were reading yourself. You are intelligent, and you know it, which is why you will use this in your favor to get an advantage in comparison with others.

You are a very curious person, and you will always show your intelligence through your discoveries.

## Aquarius Moon Weaknesses

### You Can Lose Your Temper Quickly

According to you, it is okay to explode if you must. As a result, you are happy one minute, and the next, you could curse everyone around you because you cannot stand something they had said or done.

Aquarius's temper is radical, and you are aware of this. You do not even try to hide it because you know it makes you unique.

### You are a Person Who Loves Their Distance

You need not be stuck inside a house with a person to feel you know them. You could be on the other side of the world, speaking on the phone regularly with someone you have never met in real life, yet you know who they are.

You love to keep your distance; therefore, a person under an Aquarius Moon is okay when they must move to the other side of the world without their family or friends.

### You Love Judging Others

One thing is for sure, you do not mind judging others, and you don't mind when people judge you. You point out others who make mistakes, and you will have a rough time forgetting about them.

You will also usually take your time telling others why they are failing, even if they never asked you about it.

### You Contradict Everything

It seems like your mind is constantly wandering, and some days you will say everything is white, and other days, you will say everything is black. You do not know where you are going to be every time you wake up.

This is the way you are—a contradictory person—most of the time, but you don't do it on purpose. You do it because that is just who you are.

## Aquarius Moon and Your Love Compatibility

The Aquarius Moon is someone who values his or her freedom and wants to travel the world without a return ticket. If this is your sign, chances are you want to meet someone who can keep up with you—though you know how hard that could sometimes be, especially when you are not sure where your life is heading.

Regardless of its Sun or Moon location, this sign usually has love compatibility with other fire signs (Aries, Leo, Sagittarius) or Earth Moon signs (Capricorn, Taurus, Virgo).

An Aquarius Moon needs someone who understands their need to run away but who is willing to welcome them whenever they decide to come back. You have a strong sense of humility, but you sometimes cannot reconcile your future with your present or past.

An Aquarius moon is likely going to the end of the world if it means that they will protect and defend their way of thinking. They are so stubborn that they won't even mind losing some friendships along the way if they stay committed to their truth.

An Aquarius moon is the one that seeks a travel companion, and they will find such a great soul with a Sagittarius Moon. The two will complement one another, and they will bring their best traits to the table.

It is worthy to note that an Aquarius Moon is less compatible with a Libra Moon. This combination of double air will probably make them feel bored or like they are missing something.

## Aquarius as a Sun Sign and the Different Moon Signs

### Aquarius Sun + Aries Moon

This combination is intense, and they like to get things done. Aquarius is someone who tries to understand another person's perspective, and an Aries Moon will bring other realities closer to them.

If you were born with these two signs, you are likely straightforward people who direct their flames toward solving the biggest problems they will ever encounter. They are highly independent, and it is sometimes difficult for them to allow others in and enjoy their company.

### Aquarius Sun + Taurus Moon

When these two signs are combined, they will work hard to see justice in the world, or at least within themselves. A Taurus Moon will make any Aquarius Sun work hard for what they want and need.

However, Aquarius will make the Bull work as a team, something the earth sign is not used to doing.

### Aquarius Sun + Gemini Moon

This is another double air sign pair. A person born with this combination fights for their ideals. They do not just sit down and watch the rest of the world take something on. On the contrary, if they could start a revolution by themselves, they would.

Nonetheless, a Gemini Moon will make you feel you belong to the world, and you will start feeling the need to communicate the injustices that are going on everywhere.

### Aquarius Sun + Cancer Moon

An Aquarius Sun with a Cancer Moon is someone independent who craves more independence. You may seem like an emotionally detached person when you feel something may be odd about a situation. What is more, you rely on your instinctive nature to make important decisions, and it usually works well in your favor.

Aquarius is an air sign, so having a Moon in Cancer will often make you feel more at ease when helping others. This combination is the perfect balance between being of service and staying true to oneself.

### Aquarius Sun + Leo Moon

These two signs are direct opposites on the Zodiac Chart. They will bring balance to one another, yet they will also impulse the other to get out of their comfort zone and see beyond their noses.

Having a Leo Moon means this Aquarius is ready to be at the center of the stage for a minute or two. They are not getting emotional all the time—although they may feel like their fire is ready to burst out and spread around thanks to the air sign.

**Aquarius Sun + Virgo Moon**

You do not have to look further for a more cerebral sign combination. You are the one. This does not mean you don't have a heart; it only means that you prefer to think with your head—and sometimes you prefer not to feel at all. It could be argued that emotions make you feel uncomfortable, so you avoid them.

Still, this is an interesting combination because your Aquarius Sun will make sure you stay independent. You are constantly asking yourself, "How do I serve others?" and "How can I be by myself?" if you are under this combination.

**Aquarius Sun + Libra Moon**

If you are a mixture of these two signs, you should know that everything changes and passes. You may feel confused throughout your life because these two signs are known for their wandering abilities.

You also may wonder how you can help others, but you will first need to help yourself. Your Libra Moon will show you a way, if you let it.

**Aquarius Sun + Scorpio Moon**

This is a cool and interesting combination. An Aquarius Sun tends to love a Scorpio Moon because of its depth and way of seeing life.

You are a compassionate person who is not afraid. Nothing can stop you, and you know you're a valuable resource for many individuals who look up to you. The further you go away from home, the more at peace you felt.

### Aquarius Sun + Sagittarius Moon

This is a lovely combination that is always willing to work hard to get the experience they deserve. An Aquarius Sun is someone who loves to help, and a Sagittarius Moon is the one who likes to be helped.

You will not sit still for long periods. You are very independent, and you know how much your freedom is valued because you don't know anyone else who thinks or acts like you.

### Aquarius Sun + Capricorn Moon

This combination is a powerful one because they get along very well. This Aquarius Sun will make the Capricorn Moon feel more relaxed than any other sign combinations.

An Aquarius Sun will give you a broader sense of belonging, and you will soon start noticing that there is more to life than your house or backyard.

### Aquarius Sun + Aquarius Moon

An Aquarius Sun probably has a debate with the Aquarius Moon. If this is you, you are constantly trying to prove to yourself why you need to do something instead of another thing.

You are gladly traveling away all the time, but you also feel like you are doing others a favor whenever you go away for a long time because you know they cannot handle your double air sign for long periods.

### Aquarius Sun + Pisces Moon

If you were born under this combination, you are an idealistic person who always tries to see the positive side of life. Sometimes you may feel disappointed, but you are the only one to blame, considering you put everything and everyone on a pedestal.

You are highly sensitive thanks to that Pisces Moon, yet you are also a very independent person who likes to do things their way.

# Chapter 12: Pisces Moon

**Symbol**: The Two Fishes

**Element**: Water

**Quality**: Mutable

**Ruling Planet**: Neptune

**Ruling House**: Twelfth

## A Brief Explanation of the Moon in Pisces

A Pisces Moon is someone friendly and easygoing, who loves to make others feel great about themselves. If you were born under this Moon sign, chances are you will help others when needed, without wanting to have anything back as a thank you.

Your Pisces Moon is likely making you highly sensitive to your surroundings. Everybody loves you, and you would like to love everyone back, but you are aware of the energy other people are constantly releasing. You are empathic, but you are also aware of your personal need to step back and have more room.

If you were born with this Moon sign, you are a very intuitive individual who tends to see the good in people. You love getting to know others, probably because you would like to discover whether your energies were right about that person.

You are tolerant, yet you know when to stop something, especially if it is hurting you. Not only are you the last sign of the Zodiac wheel, but you are also a mutable sign. This means you are in it for a change. You will never be the same Pisces you were a couple of days ago.

You are the one who is constantly crying when you go to your best friend's wedding and are usually called "Uncle" or "Aunt" by all your friends' kids. They love you because they know they can get a real connection from you. You are a fun friend, and children can sense this.

## Pisces Moon and Your Personality Traits

## Pisces Moon Strengths

### You are Not a Materialistic Person

Ideally, you only live with the things you truly need. You do not go out of your way to buy more things, especially when you know the space is limited.

You tend to focus on the essential value of objects. If they make you happy and are useful, you will keep them. If not, you are the first one to give everything away.

### You are Highly Sensitive

You do not mind showing your sensitive side to others, especially those closest to you. Some people may argue your authenticity, but don't worry about them, because you are one of the most compassionate signs in the Zodiac.

### You are Idealistic

You would like everything to turn out great, just like it does in your head. The difference is that you don't have an external influence when it comes to your thoughts. People will try to bring you down precisely because you focus too much on the good. You see beauty everywhere, and most people are not ready to accept this.

### You are Creative

Perhaps you are used to finding new ways to express your inner emotions because you are a mutable sign. Whether through painting, performing, or photography, you need to take everything to the next level.

You will also always influence others to follow your creative path but on their terms.

## Pisces Moon Weaknesses

### You are Pessimistic Sometimes

Being pessimistic might be very ironic, considering you are a bundle of joy most of the time, but sometimes this can get to you, and your energy levels start declining, just like the tides slow down.

If things do not work out your way, your mind will automatically start filling with pessimistic thoughts. You will continuously ask yourself what you can do differently next time around.

### You Have a Weak Character

You are only interested in what is in front of you because you are not interested in others. Sometimes people will argue you are detached from the rest of the world, and, as a result, you don't get involved in anything "serious" or worthy of your time.

Being a mutable water sign makes you wonder why other people tend to go over you. You feel disrespected, but this only occurs because you have not set your foot down and explained to others what bothers you.

**You Trust Others Too Easily**

If the first impressions are good, you are in for a ride. You will not stop trusting that person because you want to believe they arrived in your life by a stronger life force.

This could get you in trouble, especially when others do not have the same solid values you may have. You will tend to trust others the first time you meet them. Then, if things don't go according to your plans, you will wonder what you did to deserve that treatment.

**You are Too Emotional**

You are a Water Moon sign, which is the epitome of what water can accomplish. You are emotional, not afraid to admit it, and love crying and showing others that it is okay to be weak.

## Pisces Moon and Your Love Compatibility

A Pisces Moon values being emotional. They know the world would be a better place if more people would open up to their true feelings. Regardless of its Sun or Moon location, this sign usually has love compatibility with other Fire Moon signs (Aries, Leo, Sagittarius) or Earth Moon signs (Capricorn, Taurus, Virgo).

A Pisces Moon needs someone compassionate. If you were born under this Moon, you want someone to tell you it is okay to feel this way. But you also would love them to feel what you feel.

A Pisces Moon is a sensual one that is not afraid to start a new relationship. Ideally, your love could go toward an earth sign, such as a Capricorn. You two will make a great couple. For once, you will bring more passion and feelings toward your earth sign, and they will bring a more stable combination to you.

Conversely, a Pisces Moon is less compatible with another Pisces Moon. Two water signs, as well as two mutable signs, are a recipe for difficult situations. Mainly because they never know where they are heading.

## Pisces as a Sun Sign and the Different Moon Signs

### Pisces Sun + Aries Moon

If you have this powerful combination, chances are you are a very spiritual person who is always trying to light the inner fire everyone has. Moreover, this Pisces is likely bringing a fire to the equation like no other sign.

You enjoy following your instincts because you know the two opposites you have: a water sign and a fire sign.

### Pisces Sun + Taurus Moon

A Taurus Moon will bring you needed ground for you to explore, while your Pisces Sun always means that you are very empathetic toward other people. If you have this combination, you are someone who enjoys talking with others and understands the way they truly are and honors their life paths.

This combination is energetic yet flexible with everything that life throws at them. Pisces is a mutable sign, so this Moon will help Taurus become less rigid—or fixed—and become more in tune with their personal needs.

### Pisces Sun + Gemini Moon

People with these signs tend to be artists because it is such a creative combination. A Pisces Sun will allow the Gemini Moon to swim through their ideas and take them to shore to become realities.

Gemini will also allow Pisces to show them the way, something unique for the Twins, as they are used to taking the lead most of the time. A person with these signs always finds an impactful way of sharing how they feel.

**Pisces Sun + Cancer Moon**

All double water sign combinations are intense, but this one takes intensity to a whole new level. This combination can translate different types of energies in seconds. They are almost psychics when they are together.

If you were born with these signs, you are very intuitive, as they need to keep each other in balance to release old energy carried out by empathic Cancer.

**Pisces Sun + Leo Moon**

Leo loves to be at the center of the storm. Fortunately, for the fire sign, having a Pisces Sun means that they can bounce to that place, or they can completely disappear underwater.

This Pisces tends to have a stronger personality, precisely because of their Fire Moon. They are highly sensitive people who empathize with others. Yet, they still have an internal battle to fight. Who is going to win, water or fire?

**Pisces Sun + Virgo Moon**

In the Zodiac wheel, Virgo and Pisces are opposite each other. As a result, you have an inner balance that not many other signs have. You are in between the inner layers and the outer layers constantly. Your Earth Moon sign always tells you how to feel, whereas your water sign's Sun shows you how to feel.

Make sure your Virgo Moon stays in place, or you will lose your creative side, the one that reconnects you with yourself. If you remain calm and integrate these two signs, you will likely feel and be happier.

**Pisces Sun + Libra Moon**

If you were born with this combination, you have probably experienced difficult phases throughout life. First, you want to swim deep into the ocean of your thoughts. Then, you decide it is best to stay aloof, somewhere where you can see all sides.

You also have an intense emotional intuition, and you need to pay attention to it. You do not accept mistreatments or people who judge others.

**Pisces Sun + Scorpio Moon**

This is a lovely double water sign. Both Scorpio and Pisces will fight to keep the throne. Your Scorpio Moon is likely telling you where to go swimming and how to do so deeply.

Chances are you are always improving yourself. Whether this means you are succeeding academically or are inventing new things, your mind travels to new places where no one else has ever been.

**Pisces Sun + Sagittarius Moon**

A Sagittarius Moon is the one that will make your Pisces Sun feel unique. The water sign is always looking out for you. Your Pisces sign will water down your Sagittarius's fire when necessary, regardless of whether you like it or not.

However, your Sagittarius Moon is also someone who goes deeply within yourself. So, you are constantly wondering whether you should continue with your inner philosophical journey.

**Pisces Sun + Capricorn Moon**

These two signs make a lovely combination. Surprisingly, your Pisces Sun will make you go deeper within your self-healing journey. It was something you never thought would happen, but it will come to you if you allow it.

You are the one who likes to talk with family and friends for hours, nonstop. They admire you, and you are their leader, even without knowing it at times.

### Pisces Sun + Aquarius Moon

If you were born under this combination, you are an idealistic person who always tries to see the positive side of life. Sometimes you may feel disappointed, but you are the only one to blame, considering you put everything and everyone on a pedestal.

You are highly sensitive thanks to that Pisces Sun, yet you are also a very independent person who likes to do things their way, thanks to your Aquarius Moon.

### Pisces Sun + Pisces Moon

This is the last double water and double mutable sign. What a life you may have. You are intense, strong, adaptable, and enthusiastic about changes.

You probably get bored easily and need to invest your energies in new things or knowledge constantly. Watch out, though—too much water can cause severe floods.

# Conclusion

Your Moon sign is an essential piece in your self-discovery journey. Those interested in astrology and who have studied the Moon sign's influence are aware that the moon influences a person's decision. However, the Moon also tells you how to feel or makes you feel at home, most of the time.

The Moon is the one that governs your "inner self", and you need to have this information to see what makes you happy and unique. Your Moon sign will explain who you are on a deeper level, what you need to work on, and why you need to do so.

Your Moon sign will also expose your Sun sign's strengths and weaknesses. It will go after the Sun, asking why they reacted a certain way or told you to do something different from what the Moon ordered.

But it will also give you a new dynamic that you had not thought about because when your Sun and Moon are mixed, they complement you. Moreover, the Moon will change shapes within a cycle–that lasts more than twenty-seven days–so it will go from Full Moon to waxing and waning phases, to crescent phases, to finally become invisible when it is the New Moon phase.

This will have a profound impact on the decisions you make and your mood. If you are a woman, this could even affect your menstrual period. Consequently, the Moon is bound to change you in different ways throughout one single month. What is more, there is a gravitational force present in nature: when the Moon is closest to the Earth, the ocean's tides will grow exponentially.

From a broader perspective, it can be argued that the Sun is the male energy, the predominant one and father figure that goes out of its way to shine a light even in the darkest of areas. Whereas the Moon is associated with feminine energy, is a mother-like figure, and represents nature and how nature's cycles go about. The Sun represents logical thinking, while the Moon represents raw feelings. The Sun sign is the first to act toward something, where the Moon sign will react toward something.

The essential thing to know is that all human beings have an innate female and male energy. They are like yin and yang; everyone has both colors. However, society teaches that you need to choose one and focus on that person.

However, if you are a male, you also have subtle female energy that you need to nurture. If you're a female, you, too, have subtle male energy you need to take care of. The importance here is to find a balance between these two energies and discover it through your Sun and Moon signs.

Yet, this is not to say that one sign is more important than the other. On the contrary, it is impossible to determine the one that affects an individual the most.

Both signs are mutually dependent on one another. It almost seems like there is a strong gravitational force that makes the two signs work together.

If you are looking into ways of having a deeper inner connection and understanding your feelings and overall reactions and actions, have a look at your Moon sign.

If your Moon sign is the same as your Sun sign, this means you were born under a New Moon when the sky was completely dark and welcoming you.

On the other hand, if your Moon sign is directly opposite your Sun sign, it means you were born under a Full Moon. So, instead of separating yourself from others, you are bringing everything closer together.

In the astrology world, knowing your Moon sign is paramount to learning more about your birth chart. Your emotional personality is presented throughout your Moon sign. If you were to focus on your Sun sign constantly, you would discover one side of your energy, the male energy. You would also be leaving behind some relevant information about your feminine side.

But a Moon sign can also explain why sometimes you act under a cardinal, fixed, or mutable sign's perspective. Perhaps your Sun is fixed, but your Moon is mutable, so you seek inner change intensively.

When these energies collide, they will shape your personality. However, you need to become aware of them to make these energies work alongside you. If not, the signs' traits will work and play whenever they want to do so. It would be best to work on your Birth Chart with someone who knows and can guide you. Otherwise, chances are you will get confused with all the information that you can discover.

Think of the chart as an onion. The Sun sign is the first layer, the one you can easily take off. The second layer is the Moon sign. The third and fourth layers are the rest of the information you have in your chart.

Every single Zodiac sign is unique, and if you add a Moon sign to that equation, you are now in it for a treat because there are 144 combinations for people to choose from—or for the Universe to choose you as a representative life force.

This book should have given you plenty of insight into how the Zodiac Sun and Moon signs can work together to form a healthy, loving, and caring person . . . that is, you.

Welcome to this new journey. Hopefully, your Moon sign is ready to reveal some truths about yourself that you have probably left forgotten in the darkest area of your brain, heart, and soul. Ideally, your Sun sign will help you bring some light to those areas. This way, you will continue your healing path.

# Here's another book by Mari Silva that you might like

## Your Free Gift (only available for a limited time)

Thanks for getting this book! If you want to learn more about various spirituality topics, then join Mari Silva's community and get a free guided meditation MP3 for awakening your third eye. This guided meditation mp3 is designed to open and strengthen ones third eye so you can experience a higher state of consciousness. Simply visit the link below the image to get started.

https://spiritualityspot.com/meditation

# References

*Astrostyle: Astrology and Daily, Weekly, Monthly Horoscopes by The AstroTwins.* (2016). Astrostyle: Astrology and Daily, Weekly, Monthly Horoscopes by The AstroTwins. https://astrostyle.com

Faragher, A. K. (n.d.). *What Your Moon Sign Reveals About Your Emotional Personality.* Allure. Retrieved from https://www.allure.com/story/zodiac-moon-sign-emotional-personality

*Sun Signs, Astrology And Everything Else You Will Love | SunSigns.org.* (n.d.). Sun Signs. https://www.sunsigns.org/

*The Fundamental Differences Between your Sun and Moon Sign - Astroyogi.com.* (n.d.). Www.Astroyogi.com. Retrieved from https://www.astroyogi.com/articles/the-fundamental-differences-between-your-sun-and-moon-sign.aspx

*Well+Good | Your Healthiest Relationship.* (n.d.). Well+Good. Retrieved from https://www.wellandgood.com

7 Ways Understanding Your Zodiac Sign's Element Can Affect Your Horoscope. (n.d.). Bustle. https://www.bustle.com/life/7-ways-the-element-of-your-zodiac-sign-affects-your-life-why-its-so-important-to-understand-8728690

https://www.astrology.com/zodiac-signs/aries

Aquarius: Aquarius Sign Dates, Traits & More. (2017, September 25). Astrology.Com. https://www.astrology.com/zodiac-signs/aquarius

Aries Zodiac Sign Facts, Traits, Money and Compatibility | SunSigns.Org. (2019, February 19). Sun Signs. https://www.sunsigns.org/aries-zodiac-sign/

astrologer, M. H. M. H. is an, Reader, T., & Hall, author of "Astrology: A. C. I. G. to the Z. " our editorial process M. (n.d.-a). Retrieved from https://www.liveabout.com

Cabral, C. (n.d.-a). https://blog.prepscholar.com/

Cancer Sign: Cancer Zodiac Dates & Traits. (2017, September 25). Astrology.Com. https://www.astrology.com/zodiac-signs/cancer

Cancer Zodiac Sign Facts, Traits, Money and Compatibility | SunSigns.Org. (2019, February 21). Sun Signs. https://www.sunsigns.org/cancer-zodiac-sign/

Douglas, M. (n.d.). The Fundamental 6 Pisces Traits, Explained. Blog.Prepscholar.Com. Retrieved from https://blog.prepscholar.com/pisces-traits

Faragher, A. K. (n.d.). Each Zodiac Sign's Unique Personality Traits, Explained by an Astrologer. Allure. Retrieved from https://www.allure.com/story/zodiac-sign-personality-traits-dates

February 29, 2020, & Stapleton, D. (n.d.). Capricorn Zodiac Sign: Characteristics, Dates, & More. Www.Astrology.Com. Retrieved https://www.astrology.com/zodiac-signs/capricorn

Gemini Zodiac Sign Facts, Traits, Money and Compatibility | SunSigns.Org. (2019, February 21). Sun Signs. https://www.sunsigns.org/gemini-zodiac-sign/

Leo: Leo Zodiac Sign Dates, Traits & More. (2017, September 25). Astrology.Com. https://www.astrology.com/zodiac-signs/leo

Leo Zodiac Sign Facts, Traits, Money and Compatibility | SunSigns.Org. (2019, February 21). Sun Signs. https://www.sunsigns.org/leo-zodiac-sign/

Libra Sign Dates, Traits, & More. (2017, September 25). Astrology.Com. https://www.astrology.com/zodiac-signs/libra

Logan, B. (n.d.-a). https://blog.prepscholar.com/aries-traits-personality

May 14, 2020, & Stapleton, D. (n.d.). Scorpio Zodiac Sign: Characteristics, Dates, & More. Www.Astrology.Com. Retrieved https://www.astrology.com/zodiac-signs/scorpio

Muniz, H. (n.d.-b). The 7 Aquarius Traits You Need to Know. Blog.Prepscholar.Com. https://blog.prepscholar.com/aquarius-traits-personality

Muniz, H. (n.d.-c). The 7 Fundamental Cancer Traits and What They Mean for You. Blog.Prepscholar.Com. Retrieved https://blog.prepscholar.com/cancer-traits-personality

Pisces Zodiac Sign Facts, Traits, Money and Compatibility | SunSigns.Org. (2019, February 22). Sun Signs. https://www.sunsigns.org/pisces-zodiac-sign/

Robinson, A. (n.d.-a). The 5 Fundamental Sagittarius Traits You Need to Know. Blog.Prepscholar.Com. https://blog.prepscholar.com/sagittarius-traits-personality

Robinson, A. (n.d.-b). The 8 Key Leo Traits: Your Guide to the August Zodiac Sign. Blog.Prepscholar.Com. https://blog.prepscholar.com/leo-traits-personality

Sagittarius Zodiac Sign Facts, Traits, Money, Compatibility | SunSigns.Org. (2019, February 22). Sun Signs. https://www.sunsigns.org/sagittarius-zodiac-sign/

Scorpio Zodiac Sign Facts, Traits, Money and Compatibility | SunSigns.Org. (2019, February 22). Sun Signs. https://www.sunsigns.org/scorpio-zodiac-sign/

Seigel, D. (2016). The 7 Fundamental Gemini Traits, Explained. Prepscholar.Com. https://blog.prepscholar.com/gemini-traits

Sun in Aquarius Sign: Meaning, Significance And Personality Traits | SunSigns.Org. (2014, September 15). Sun Signs. https://www.sunsigns.org/sun-in-aquarius/

Taurus Zodiac Sign Facts, Traits, Money and Compatibility | SunSigns.Org. (2019, February 21). Sun Signs. https://www.sunsigns.org/taurus-zodiac-sign/

Virgo Zodiac Sign Facts, Traits, Money and Compatibility | SunSigns.Org. (2019, February 21). Sun Signs. https://www.sunsigns.org/virgo-zodiac-sign/

What Does Your Sun, Moon, and Rising Sign Really Mean? (n.d.). Mindbody. https://explore.mindbodyonline.com/blog/wellness/what-does-your-sun-moon-and-rising-sign-really-mean

What's The Difference Between Your Sun, Moon & Rising Signs? An Astrology Explainer. (n.d.). Bustle. https://www.bustle.com/p/whats-the-difference-between-your-sun-moon-rising-signs-astrology-explainer-38066

CPSIA information can be obtained
at www.ICGtesting.com
Printed in the USA
LVHW080303220721
693389LV00001B/2